M000080146

According to Your Word

MORNING AND EVENING THROUGH THE NEW TESTAMENT

STEPHEN F. OLFORD

A COLLECTION OF DEVOTIONAL JOURNALS 1940-1941

B&H
PUBLISHING GROUP

NASHVILLE, TENNESSEE

According to Your Word: Morning and
Evening through the New Testament
© 2008 Heather Olford
All rights reserved.
ISBN: 978-08054-4549-7

B&H Publishing Group
Nashville, Tennessee
BHPublishingGroup.com

Dewey Decimal Classification: 242.5
Subject Headings:
Devotional Literature/Bible N.T.—Study

Printed in the USA
1 2 3 4 5   12 11 10 09 08

Dedicated to the Olford grandchildren:

Jeremy, Justin, Joshua,
Lindsay, and Stephanie

With our prayers that you will
love and live according to His Word.

How can a young man
cleanse his way?

By taking heed
according to Your word.

Psalm 119:9

Writing the Preface to introduce this collection of devotional thoughts by my husband is both a great joy and a great privilege. Stephen Olford was a man of prayer and devotion to God's Word, and thus it was not a surprise to discover this material after he died in 2004. Most of these devotionals were written from 1940 to 1941, when Stephen was in his twenties and London was experiencing the bombings of World War Two. I believe their focus, depth, and insight reveal just how valuable it is to spend time with God, no matter your age or circumstances.

If I may, let me tell you a bit about Stephen. Born in 1918 in Africa, Stephen, as well as his brothers Paul and John, grew up in Angola in a missionary home with their godly parents. He grew into a mature young man who came to know Christ as his Savior at the age of seven and watched the blessings of his parents, Fred and Bessie, as they preached and showed the love of God to people who mostly had never heard the Gospel.

In 1935, when Stephen was seventeen, the Olford family returned to England. He had a difficult time adjusting, particularly to a church that was not spiritually alive or helpful to someone his age. Stephen went through a time of doubt and sought his own path for life as he studied engineering in Plymouth, England. But God had other plans for him. As a result of injuries received in a motorcycle accident, Stephen came face to face with death, but through the faithful prayers of his parents and the touch of a loving God, he was healed both physically and spiritually.

Stephen's heart was changed and set on serving his Lord. He was accepted to study at St. Luke's College in London and from there he went to the Missionary Training Colony, also in London. Missions and missionaries had been his world all his life, and he so wanted to prepare for that as best as he could.

As a student, one of the great lessons Stephen learned was the blessing of time spent every day alone with God, his Bible, and in prayer – the secrets of the "Quiet Time." I often heard him tell how surprised he was to discover that each student at the Missionary Colony was expected to spend one to two hours quietly every morning in prayer and the reading of God's Word. At first, he wondered what on earth he would do for that long. But he soon learned that those hours spent alone with God were all too short and were times of learning the deep truths of his faith and love for God.

In fact, some of these precious quiet times would later become sermons that were preached all over the world. Some years later, when Stephen was preaching at Moody Bible College, he challenged students to make a time for God each day. God used that message to bring revival to the campus, and it was from this sermon that the booklet, *Manna in the Morning*, was written.

Almost from the moment we met in 1947, I have loved this man because God's love shone through every part of his life. Our hearts and lives were knit together and we were married in 1948. For fifty-six years, we served "together with God" raising a family, ministering in the pastorate, and teaching other pastors. Stephen was a godly, holy man. I invite you to read *The Life and Legacy of Stephen Olford* by John Phillips to learn more about my husband and his ministry.

My many thanks must go to Broadman and Holman Publishing Group, and Anita Bosley for her careful preparation of these daily meditations. It is my prayer that as you read these pages—as well as the entire chapters of the Bible referenced in each entry—you will be blessed and encouraged to spend time in quiet meditation day by day.

From David Olford

Just after the Second World War, sensing a deep spiritual hunger, my father was refreshed and revived during a time of personal retreat with the Lord. Shortly thereafter, he met Billy Graham (1946). Due to young Billy Graham's similar spiritual hunger, the two arranged to meet in Wales for a time of retreat together. It is my understanding that one of the subjects discussed during this time together was the devotional life or the "quiet time."

According to Your Word reveals that the "quiet time" was already a discipline in my father's life before this important meeting in 1946. These devotionals are evidence of a thoughtful and prayerful reading of the Word of God that was (and would be) a regular feature of my father's life.

My father practiced the quiet time until his death at age eighty-six. His sudden departure reminds me of the Scriptural account of Enoch who "walked with God; and he was not, for God took him" (Gen. 5:24). We miss Dad greatly, but we know that his walk with God continues above.

My dad was my hero and the depth of his spiritual walk as a young man, as evidenced in this thoughtful journey through the Scriptures, draws attention to his love of the Word of God and his desire to spend his life walking in the footsteps of His Lord and Savior Jesus Christ – living *According to Your Word*. This book is a study in the application of God's Word during a time defined as "a world at war." However, while the nature of the war has changed and the era these meditations were written in has long since passed, our world today is just as tumultuous and filled with ongoing horror, pain, and suffering. These readings are as relevant today as they were when they were written nearly seventy years ago.

It is my prayer that as you read these devotional thoughts you will be drawn into a closer walk with Jesus, that you would find strength, comfort, and challenge in His Word, and that you would similarly experience the energy, devotion, and commitment of a true man of God, my dad, Stephen Olford.

"Do not be afraid to take to you Mary your wife, for that which is conceived in her is of the Holy Spirit."
— *Matthew 1:20*

Until this declaration by the angel, Joseph was ashamed, afraid, and apologetic. He was ashamed because of the apparent embarrassment into which he had been plunged; he was afraid to go through with the solemn vows previously made; he was apologetic in trying to explain away the great mistake; and he resolved to divorce her quietly. "But while he thought about these things, behold, an angel of the Lord appeared" (v. 20). This made all the difference.

When God manifestly reveals that a certain thing or procedure is of the Holy Spirit, there are only three things to be done:

Stand fast. "Take to you Mary your wife." In other words, stand by all your original vows and decisions. *Shun fear.* "Do not be afraid." Whatever man may or may not say must not distract or distress. *Show faith.* "That . . . is of the Holy Spirit." Demonstrate without apology that Christ is in and with you.

Lord, You have spoken; give me grace to obey. Amen.

*"When they ... saw the young Child ... [they] fell down
and worshiped Him." – Matthew 2:11*

Paul says, "Great is the mystery of godliness:
God was manifested in the flesh" (1 Tim. 3:16).
"The young Child" – God manifest in the
flesh!

Is it any wonder the wise men worshipped?
They "fell down and worshipped Him." Notice
how often men fell at the feet of Jesus:

- "They ... fell down" at His birth (v. 11).
- "They fell on their faces" at His
  Transfiguration (Matt. 17:6).
- They fell down and "held Him by the
  feet" at His Resurrection (Matt. 28:9).
- "I fell at His feet as dead" – at His
  Glorification (Rev. 1:17).

There are even more occasions, but at each
they fell in worship, wonder, and awe.

*Lord, give me these visions by faith,
that I may similarly worship.*

"It is fitting for us to fulfill all righteousness."
— Matthew 3:15

The word "righteousness" here means "rightness" or "justice." The standard of the Lord Jesus Christ (right through His life) was to fulfill *right*. At twelve years of age, He is heard to say, "Did you not know that I must be about My Father's business?" (Luke 2:49). When He uttered the words here in Matthew, the Lord Jesus was just about to step out on His three and half years of public ministry and His standard was still the fulfilling of righteousness (the will of God).

A little later on, He says, "My food is to do the will of Him who sent Me, and to finish His work" (John 4:34). Then, towards the end, "I have finished the work which You have given Me to do" (John 17:4). Then finally, "It is finished" (John 19:30). He fulfilled *"all"* righteousness." But notice also, He says, "It is fitting for *us*." Surely, this is what the apostle directs when he writes, "Walk worthy [becomingly] of the calling with which you were called" (Eph. 4:1).

Lord, help me to walk worthily,
that I might fulfill all righteousness.

"It is written . . ." — Matthew 4:4, 7, 10

How wonderfully the Lord Jesus wielded the sword of the Spirit on this occasion!

There is obviously great significance in the fact that Christ met this temptation (and the tempter) with the Word of God. The apostle John, in his first epistle, writes to the young men because they were strong, the Word of God abode in them, and they had overcome the wicked one. Revelation 12:11 says, "They overcame him [the Devil] by the blood of the Lamb and by the word of their testimony." Here, in Matthew, are three instances at least where the Word of God is definitely regarded as the only successful weapon against the Devil (notice also Ephesians 6). The blood of the Lamb, of course, is the only basis upon which the Word can be rightly used.

Lord, may the Word abide in me.
Amen.

MORNING READING: MATTHEW 5

"Blessed are the pure in heart,
for they shall see God." – Matthew 5:8

The word "pure" can mean "clean," "pure" or
"clear." Happy are the clean in heart for they
shall see God. "How can a young man cleanse
his way? By taking heed according to Your
word" (Ps. 119:9). The Lord Jesus said on one
occasion to His disciples, "You are already
clean because of the word which I have
spoken to you" (John 15:3). In that wonderful
prayer of His, He says, "Sanctify them by Your
truth. Your word is truth" (John 17:17).

God demands holiness – "Be holy, for I am
holy" (1 Peter 1:16).

O Lord, allow the cleansing Blood, the cleansing Word,
and the cleansing Hope by the operation of the Holy
Spirit to make me pure "just as He is pure" (1 John 3:3).

*"For where your treasure is, there your
heart will be also."* — Matthew 6:21

How necessary then to "lay up . . . treasures in
heaven" (v. 20). The apostle Paul expresses the
same truth when he says, "Storing up for
themselves a good foundation for the time to
come, that they may lay hold on eternal life"
(1 Tim. 6:19).

It would seem from the last quoted Scripture
and its context, that *laying up treasure* really
means:

- "Trust in the living God" (1 Tim. 4:10)
- Readiness to give of your riches
  (1 Tim. 6:18)

But, as to heaven, *laying up treasure* means:

- A good foundation for the future
  (1 Tim. 6:19)
- A laying hold of eternal life
  (1 Tim. 6:19)

This is the real treasure – the center of heart
affections.

*May I set my affections on things above, Lord,
and not on things of the earth. Amen.*

*"Whatever you want men to do to you,
do also to them."* — Matthew 7:12

Herein is the true Christian principle of living. It was certainly the standard the Lord Jesus set when here upon earth, for He lived a life of self-abnegation. "Even Christ did not please Himself" (Rom. 15:3). Christ spent, and was spent, entirely on others. With that standard in view, the apostle writes, "Let each of us please his neighbor for his good, leading to edification" (Rom. 15:2), "Be kindly affectionate to one another with brotherly love, in honor giving preference to one another" (Rom. 12:10), "Be of the same mind toward one another" (Rom. 12:16), "For none of us lives to himself" (Rom. 14:7). In fact, the trend of all the teaching of the Epistles has this principle intertwined in it.

*Work this principle into my life by
Your Holy Spirit, O Lord. Amen.*

~

Evening Reading: Matthew 8

"Only speak a word." — *Matthew 8:8*

"The word of God is living and powerful,
and sharper than any two-edged sword"
(Heb. 4:12).

He brought the worlds into existence by
speaking a Word. He upholds all things by the
Word of His power. He spoke and the dead
were raised. At His Word, men and women
were healed.

Even though it was faith that revealed it to
him, it is a wonder that this man could utter
such a statement: "Only speak a word." Peter
likewise, on one occasion, had to set aside
experience and knowledge and by faith say,
"Nevertheless at Your word" (Luke 5:5).
People marveled at the gracious words that
proceeded out of the Lord's mouth. He spoke
as one having authority, and not as the scribes.

*I praise You, O Lord, for Your wonderful and
powerful Word. May I trust Your Word
and act upon it more fully.*

~

"It was never seen like this." — Matthew 9:33

What a difference the presence and power of
the Lord Jesus makes! This chapter, in itself,
contains a remarkable record of Christ's
miraculous power:

- He cured one sick of the palsy.
- He cured the bloody issue.
- He raised Jairus' daughter.
- He gave sight to the two blind men.
- He cast the Devil out of the dumb man.

This amazing demonstration of power called
forth, from the marveling multitudes, the very
true statement and testimony: "It was never
seen like this." And yet, there is no limit to the
power of the Lord Jesus. It is beyond man's
finite comprehension. What He did in each of
these five cases recorded here, He can do in
the life of any man. In fact, to use the words of
another, "It is yet to be seen what God can do
with the man . . . wholly surrendered to Him."

What joy the promise of my Savior:
"You will see greater things than these" (John 1:50).

*"Do not worry about how or what you should speak.
For it will be given to you in that hour what you should
speak; for it is not you who speak, but the Spirit of your
Father who speaks in you." — Matthew 10:19-20*

Personally, I feel that in these two verses is a
principle that should always operate in public
speaking. By that, I mean that the inference
here is not exclusively for the servant of the
Lord who is delivered up. Notice also,
"Behold, I have put My words in your mouth"
(Jer. 1:9); "The Spirit of the LORD spoke by
me, And His word was on my tongue"
(2 Sam. 23:2); "I will be with your mouth
and teach you what you shall say" (Ex. 4:12).
These are just a few of the many instances
where the above principle obviously operates.

Speak in living echoes of Your tone.

"I am gentle and lowly in heart." – Matthew 11:29

Notice that it expressly says: "Lowly in *heart*." God had to say of His people Israel that they honored Him with their *lips*, but their *hearts* were far from Him. God only recognizes what comes directly from the heart. Hence, we hear Him, who was the Perfect Man before God saying, "I am . . . lowly in heart."

He Was Lowly in What He Became. For though the Son of God, "He humbled Himself" (Phil. 2:8). "He became poor" (2 Cor. 8:9). He became man.

He Was Lowly in What He Said. "I do nothing of Myself" (John 8:28). "I am gentle and lowly" (Matt. 11:29). "The Son of Man has nowhere to lay His head" (Matt. 8:20).

He Was Lowly in What He Did. He sat and ate with sinners, identified Himself with all who were poor or diseased, and finally died a shameful death.

Do that which is necessary, Lord,
to keep me lowly in heart.

*"For out of the abundance of the heart
the mouth speaks." — Matthew 12:34*

It is interesting to note how many times the
Lord charged those upon whom He had
performed some miracle of healing not to
publish the fact abroad. But in most cases, if
not in all, it seems that the persons concerned
could not control themselves. One reads over
and over again that they proclaimed the news
freely. It was a case of "For out of the
abundance of the heart the mouth speaks."

Similarly, it is only when grace does a real
work in the heart, only when the heart is full
of the Holy Spirit (Eph. 5:18), only when
Christ is all in all, that the mouth will speak.

*Lord, I will testify of Your goodness and grace
out of the abundance of my heart.*

*"He did not do many mighty works there because
of their unbelief." — Matthew 13:58*

What an amazing, yet solemn, verse this is!
*Purge me, O Lord, that I may never be guilty of
such unbelief!*

Notice that the verse does not say, "He *could*
not," but rather that "He *did* not." It was not a
case that His power was limited on this
particular occasion, but rather that Christ does
not work in the presence of blatant or open
unbelief.

Unbelief is the preeminent fruit of the flesh.
It is that which emanates from man's corrupt
nature. "The carnal mind is enmity against
God" (Rom. 8:7).

*Give me the grace to crucify the natural man
in me, Lord, until all unbelief is removed.*

"They do not need to go away." — Matthew 14:16

The disciples said, "Send the multitudes away" (v. 15). Jesus said, "They do not need to go away." Herein is seen the very heart of my blessed Lord. The flesh in me would rather be unburdened of the responsibility of feeding the hungering, perishing multitude, even though the day of opportunity is drawing to a close (notice that it was evening). But the Lord essentially said, "They do not need to go away. They can go if they wish to. They must go if you force them. But as far as I am concerned, they do not have to go away." In fact, they were fed: "You give them something to eat" (v. 16).

"They do not need to go away" (v. 16). "The one who comes to Me I will by no means cast out" (John 6:37).

Give me this spirit, Lord!

Morning Reading: Matthew 15

"Down at Jesus' feet." — Matthew 15:30

What a blessed place is this! O, to be found continually at His feet! Being "down at Jesus' feet" is:

A *Place of Healing.* We read here that the *lame* – those who could not walk; the *blind* – those who could not see; the *dumb* – those who could not talk; the *maimed* – those who could not work, all were cast down with many others at Jesus' feet. "Cast . . . down" (Matt. 15:30, KJV) means to be thrown down in all their worthlessness and helplessness – and Jesus healed them!

A *Place of Learning.* "Mary . . . sat at Jesus' feet and heard His word" (Luke 10:39). The Lord spoke of this as more needful than much serving. Oh, to be found here.

A *Place of Worship.* "They came and held Him by the feet and worshiped Him." (Matt. 28:9). The disciples had met the risen Lord and He had said, "Rejoice!" (v. 9), and they worshiped.

At Your feet is a blessed place, Lord.
O, to be found continually there!

"He turned and said to Peter, 'Get behind Me,
Satan! You are an offense to Me.'"
— Matthew 16:23

Not half a dozen verses previous to this, in
reply to Peter's great statement concerning
Christ: "You are the Christ, the Son of the
living God" (v. 16), the Lord was saying to
Peter, "Blessed are you, Simon Bar–Jonah, for
flesh and blood has not revealed this to you,
but My Father who is in heaven" (v. 17). But
He who was the Light, is, and ever will be the
Light, never covered wrong at the expense of
His holiness. So when he detects the work of
the Devil in what, humanly speaking, was
loving sympathy on the part of Peter, the Lord
strictly rebukes him.

O Lord, make me this consistent.
Amen.

"Nevertheless, lest we offend them, go to the sea, cast in a hook." – Matthew 17:27

In this verse, the Lord practices his own teaching on offending, and takes every step to avoid offense.

Some of the most severe language the Lord ever used in His teaching was in connection with the offending of little ones. "Whoso shall offend one of these little ones which believe in me, it were better for him, that a millstone were hanged about his neck, and that he were drowned in the depth of the sea" (Matt. 18:6, KJV).

The apostle Paul similarly teaches this important truth, and indeed more – he lived it. He says that even if it were merely in the eating of meat that he made his brother to offend, he would cease to eat altogether. Note the solemn words in 1 Cor. 8:12: "When you thus sin against the brethren, and wound their weak conscience, you sin against Christ."

O, that I might have the wisdom to live a life without offense, and yet not compromise Your Holy Word.

"So My heavenly Father also will do to you if each of you, from his heart, does not forgive his brother his trespasses."
— *Matthew 18:35*

Here is certainly strong language! How can the believer read such a verse and not see to it that he has a forgiving spirit?

The apostle Paul teaches the same truth. He says, "Be kind to one another, tenderhearted [corresponding with *his heart* in the verse above], forgiving one another, just as God in Christ forgave you" (Eph. 4:32).

And John: "Whoever hates his brother is a murderer" (1 John 3:15).

Thus, a forgiving spirit is essential. In fact, it is the positive fruit of one born of God. In another place, it is given as the condition for prevailing prayer.

O Lord, cultivate in me the same forgiving spirit You have shown me.

"If you want to be perfect, go, sell what you have and give to the poor, and you will have treasure in heaven; and come, follow Me." — Matthew 19:21

The Lord's desire for this young man was that he might prove not only the *good* and *acceptable* will of God, but also the *perfect* will of God. "If you want to be perfect." What then had the young man to do?

William Cowper had to say from a heart experience:

> The dearest idol I have known,
> Whate'er that idol be
> Help me to tear it from Thy throne,
> And worship only Thee.[1]

What the Lord wanted from this young man was not his riches so much, but the unreserved surrender of his heart and body. Instead, he chose the fleeting treasures of time in place of the pleasures of eternity. He denied himself the possession of eternal life for the temporary enjoyment of earthly riches.

Continue to remind me, Lord,
to strive for Your perfect will in my life.

"Is it not lawful for me to do what I wish with my own things?" — Matthew 20:15

This parable preeminently sets forth the spirit of humility and the sense of unworthiness that should characterize the servant of God. The servant should always remember that even after he has done all, he is unprofitable, for he has only then done his rightful duty.

Moreover, "Shall not the Judge of all the earth do right?" (Gen. 18:25). Who is the servant to question His justice?

It is very obvious that the grumbling servants of this parable were more concerned about their pay than about their faithfulness to the landowner who had called them into service, for no other reason than the fact that he was full of grace and kindness. Who am I? Why should I be called – let alone chosen – to serve God, when thousands are not? This must be our spirit.

Lord, I am humbled that You would call me to serve You.

"He was hungry." — Matthew 21:18

Truly, great is the mystery of godliness –
God was manifested in the flesh! That He, the
Jehovah Jireh, should hunger is a mystery that
baffles the finite mind.

Yet it is a precious thought and fact. For
having passed the way of all men, He can now
be touched with every feeling of my infirmity.
Having been tested, He can now succor.

Yes, my blessed Lord hungered, slept, wearied,
wept, sorrowed, suffered, and died – Praise
His wonderful Name!

Give me the power and grace, O Lord, to walk
even as You did walk in this scene despite the fact
that You were perfectly human. Amen.

"Jesus answered and spoke to them . . . by parables."
— Matthew 22:1

Someone has said, "A parable is an earthly story with a heavenly meaning."

In any case, the Lord Jesus in His preaching and teaching made great use of parables. Their purpose was to illuminate the truth to those who were ready to receive it, and to conceal the truth to those who were unbelieving.

The Lord Jesus used everyday life and common scenes to build His stories. He adapted Himself to His audiences and circumstances.

His three great study books were God's Book, the Book of Creation, and the Book of Human Life.

Teach me, Lord, how to use these three books skillfully in my ministry for You. Amen.

"Hypocrites!" — Matthew 23:23

To those whose comprehension of God is one of love alone, what a chapter is this! Woe! Woe! Woe! Eight times, like the toll of the death bell! Who could possibly deny that God is a God of righteous judgment after reading a chapter such as this?

"But why such strong language?" the soul asks. The answer is because of the existence of hypocrisy. Hypocrisy is the greatest of all abominations before the Lord. Men who were outright sinners, the Lord called sinners and dealt with them in grace (Mark 2, John 8; 15:2, etc.). But when it came to hypocrites, the Lord scathingly denounced them. Notice in Acts 5, that even among His own people in the early Church, the Lord did not tolerate hypocrisy.

O, that I might recognize any hypocrisy in my life and deal with it swiftly and decisively!

"My master is delaying his coming."
— Matthew 24:48

It is one of the Devil's greatest achievements to perpetrate this falsehood. For falsehood it is. The Scriptures declare "The Lord is not slack concerning His promise [of His coming], as some count slackness, but is longsuffering toward us, not willing that any should perish" (2 Peter 3:9). The apostle says, "The time is short" (1 Cor. 7:29). The Lord Jesus says, "Behold, I am coming quickly" (Rev. 3:11).

Nevertheless, there are those who are controlled by their own lusts and by the Devil, who say, "Where is the promise of His coming? For since the fathers fell asleep, all things continue as . . . from the beginning" (2 Peter 3:4). The apostle replies that these people are willingly ignorant of the Word of God.

O Lord, make Your coming a living reality in my life; that the Hope may purify my heart even as You are pure.

"To each according to his own ability."
— Matthew 25:15

What an encouraging fact this is! Yet, it is one
which carries with it a real responsibility. For
"according to his own ability," the Lord
requires His portion. There is no genuine
servant of the Lord who has not been given
his talent or talents. To suggest that there is
would be to refute the Word of God and to
cast a doubt on the grace of God.

The Word declares, concerning gifts, the
"Spirit . . . [distributes] to each one
individually as He wills" (1 Cor. 12:11).
Moreover, as is emphasized in this parable,
God never expects interest from what He has
not given. It is true the slothful servant tried
to cast a doubt on the love and justice of God
by calling Him "hard" (Matt. 25:24), but his
own injustice condemned him in the end.
The Lord Jesus says, "My yoke is easy"
(Matt. 11:30).

*May I be abundantly faithful with the precious gifts God
has entrusted to me, for His Name's sake. Amen.*

"Immediately he went up to Jesus and said,
'Greetings, Rabbi!' and kissed Him."
— Matthew 26:49

Darby renders this verse: "Hail, Rabbi, and covered him with kisses."[2]

What an antithesis this is to the picture in Luke 7:38. There we see a woman who had been forgiven much, expressing the true love of her heart in kissing the feet of Jesus. Covering them with kisses!

Here, in verse 49, it is not the kiss of love but the kiss of betrayal. It is inconceivable and incredible that a man who had so lived and learned of Christ could be capable of such an act of treachery. The only solution is that we read, "Satan entered him [Judas]" and he went out (John 13:27, 30).

Lord, keep me from ever betraying You with
the outward sign of love!

"Truly this was the Son of God!" — Matthew 27:54

The rest of the verse qualifies this great statement: "So when the centurion and those with him, who were guarding Jesus, saw the earthquake and the things that had happened, they feared greatly, saying, 'Truly this was the Son of God!'" (v. 54).

They watched Jesus. They saw His wonderful behavior from Gabbatha to Golgotha. They saw the "sorrow and love flow mingled down."[3] They heard His words.

They *"saw the earthquake and the things that had happened."* The veil rent in twain – two or three miles away. This was in fulfillment of His own Word. The earth did quake – the very universe trembled in His presence. The dead arose. He was Resurrection and Life.

"They feared greatly." Here was reverence, awe, and trepidation – for they were in the presence of the Son of God.

Your presence always brings reverence and awe.
Truly, You are the Son of God!

"All authority has been given to Me in heaven
and on earth." — Matthew 28:18

These are the words of the risen Christ. They
are the words of the One who could say, "I am
He who lives, and was dead, and behold, I am
alive forevermore. Amen. And I have the keys
of Hades and of Death" (Rev. 1:18).

- "All authority." This comprehends every
  power and principality.
- "Given to Me." The exalted and ever-
  living Savior.
- "In heaven and on earth." The angels
  and millions of heavenly hosts are not
  only to see the demonstration of that
  power, but also the thousands of people
  upon earth.

Therefore, says the risen Lord, "All authority
has been given to Me . . . Go" (Matt. 28:18-19).
In other words, "I have the power, I will
impart the power. You, Go."

Teach me daily how to appropriate this power.
Amen.

"There comes One after me who is mightier than I,
whose sandal strap I am not worthy to stoop down
and loose." — Mark 1:7

The stooping to unloose the strap of a sandal
was the meanest job for the lowest servant. Yet
John the Baptist says, "I am not worthy even
to do that." He says that he was not worthy
even to stoop down. Stooping down was
humility itself, but John says that he was not
worthy to take such a high place (though
humanly speaking it was the lowest place).

Here, surely, was real humility. And because
of it, the Lord exalted John the Baptist to
the highest place of honor. For He said
concerning him that John was the greatest
born of women (Matt. 11:11).

Notice also, "Whoever exalts himself will be
humbled, and he who humbles himself will
be exalted" (Matt. 23:12).

"Humble yourselves in the sight of the Lord,
and He will lift you up."
— James 4:10

"He was in the house." — Mark 2:1

What happens when Christ is in a house?
Notice the following things:

There is a Drawing Power. "Immediately many
gathered together, so that there was no longer
room to receive them" (v. 2). Wherever the
Lord Jesus is, there is drawing power. "And I, if
I am lifted up from the earth, will draw all
peoples to Myself" (John 12:32).

There is Preaching Power. "He preached the
word to them" (v. 2). Luke adds, "The power of
the Lord was present to heal them" (Luke
5:17). Paul tells me that "where the Spirit of
the Lord is, there is liberty" (2 Cor. 3:17).
When Christ is in the house, there is perfect
liberty for preaching.

There is Healing Power. To quote Luke again, he
says, "The power of the Lord was present to
heal them" (Luke 5:17). Notice also the
healing of the palsied man, and also the
forgiving of his sins.

Lord, take Your rightful place in MY house.

"He is out of His mind." — Mark 3:21

These words were said to my blessed Lord by members of His own kinsmen. It was their estimate of the loving and increasing labors of my Lord.

The Lord Jesus said on one occasion: "The night is coming when no one can work" (John 9:4). Earlier in His life, "I *must* be about My Father's business" (Luke 2:49, emphasis mine). Again, "The fields . . . are *already* white for harvest" (John 4:35, emphasis mine). In all such statements, He sought to show that time was short; opportunities must be redeemed now or never. But He not only taught this, He practiced it! Hence, He is seen in this chapter not having enough time to even eat bread. Those nearest to Him by family relationships could only find these unkind and scathing words: "He is out of His mind."

Lord, in light of these words, help me never
to be affected by derogatory criticism.

"Take heed what you hear. With the same measure you use, it will be measured to you; and to you who hear, more will be given." — Mark 4:24

Here is a very important principle in relation to the effect of God's Word in the life of an individual. "Take heed," says the Savior, for your appreciation of and obedience to the Word of God governs its effect in life and also governs any further revelation.

The same principle is seen in Hebrews 5:12-14 and 1 Corinthians 3:1-4, where the apostle shows that owing to disobedience on the part of those who heard the Word, they had not grown sufficiently to be able to bear a heavier diet. They were unskillful, only taking milk. "Take heed" is the command and secret of growth.

May I always listen and respond to the Word of God, and thus grow, for Your glory, Lord. Amen.

*"The woman, fearing and trembling, knowing
what had happened to her, came and fell down
before Him and told Him the whole truth."*
— Mark 5:33

Nothing is hidden from "the eyes of Him to
whom we must give account" (Heb. 4:13). All
things are open and naked. This woman was
conscious of this fact, so she told Him the
whole truth. This confession brought her
heart peace and she went away happy.
The only real secret of peace lies in the
unburdening of the heart to God.

Acts 5 records the story of two who "kept
back" that which they professed before man
to have given to God (v. 2). Man might have
taken it as the whole truth, but not so God.
The result of this deceit was death.

First John 1:9 says, "If we confess our sins, He
is faithful and just to forgive us our sins and to
cleanse us from all unrighteousness."

Lord, help me to be honest and open before You.

*"They were greatly amazed in themselves beyond
measure, and marveled. For they had not understood
about the loaves, because their heart was hardened."*
— Mark 6:51-52

The Lord Jesus, prior to this incident, had fed
five thousand people with five loaves and two
small fishes. It was a miracle calculated to
beget faith in any heart. But it evidently made
little impression on the disciples. Had they
considered the miracle of the loaves, they would
have recognized Christ's omnipotence. Had
they *considered* Christ as the Sustainer and
Upholder, they would have recognized Him
as the Creator, and therefore Master of the
elements. But no, their hearts were hardened.
Hebrews teaches that the hardened heart of
unbelief comes through departing from the
Living God through the deceitfulness
of sin.

*Lord, may I never harden my heart
to the point that I fail to consider Your hand
in the world around me.*

Morning Reading: Mark 7

"He could not be hidden." — Mark 7:24

Wherever Christ is given His rightful place, He cannot be hidden, for He is the *Light* of the world and therefore, a *Light* which cannot be hidden. Christ is the "the true Light which gives light to every man coming into the world" (John 1:9).

"He could not be hidden." This was also said of Peter and John, for it is recorded that when people saw them, they took knowledge of them that they had been with Jesus. Paul's great ambition was that Christ should *live* in him. He could say, "It is no longer I who live, but Christ lives in me" (Gal. 2:20).

The Lord said in that wonderful sermon of His, "Let your light so shine . . . that they . . . glorify your Father" (Matt. 5:16).

O, that this might be said of my life!

"You are the Christ." — Mark 8:29

This testimony of Peter was not the result of human reasoning or even imagination, but as the Lord Himself says, "The revelation of the Father" (see Matt. 16:17). And what a revelation it was, for Peter recognized in Christ:

An Anointed Prophet. That is to say, a Teacher sent from God. He saw in Him "the way, the truth, and the life" (John 14:6). Peter himself said on one occasion, "Lord, to whom shall we go? *You* have the words of eternal life" (John 6:68, emphasis mine).

An Anointed Priest. One sent from God to mediate between God and Man.

An Anointed King. Peter probably recognized Him as King more than in any other capacity. What a revelation Peter must have had!

You are the Christ — Prophet, Priest, and King!
Amen.

MORNING READING: MARK 9

"Only Jesus." — Mark 9:8

Had it been "only Moses," they would have
had to face the severe demands of the law.
Had it been "only Elias," they would have had
to suffer the righteous demands of severe
judgment. But it was "Only Jesus!" Blessed be
His Name! "Only Jesus," who not only
fulfilled the law but also bore the judgment
due to mankind, that as "The Only Savior" He
might bring "grace and truth" (John 1:14, 17)
to men and women. Had *only* Moses and Elias
come down, they would have brought law and
judgment. But in that "Only Jesus" came
down, He brought truth (fulfilled law) and
grace (satisfied judgment). Praise God for
"Only Jesus!"

Jesus is All the world to me,
My life, my joy, my all;
He is my strength from day to day,
Without Him I would fall.[4]
"Only Jesus" (Mark 9:8).

EVENING READING: MARK 10

"Who then can be saved?" — Mark 10:26

The Lord Jesus had just made three important
statements, which represented in themselves
three possible stages in the experience of an
unsaved man. They were:

"How hard it is for those who have riches" to be
saved (v. 23)! Here the possession of riches is
best illustrated in the foregoing story of the
rich young ruler. "He . . . went away sorrowful,
for he had great possessions" (v. 22).

"How hard it is for those who trust in riches" to be
saved (v. 24)! Here is not merely possession of,
but "trust in," riches. This is illustrated by
Paul's words in 1 Timothy 6:17: "Command
those who are rich . . . not to . . . trust in
uncertain riches but in the living God."

*"It is easier for a camel to go through the eye of a
needle than for a rich man"* to be *saved* (v. 25)!
Here is the "love of riches" to the exclusion of
all else (God) (see also Luke 12:16-21).

*However, with You, Father,
even such as these can be saved.*

"Have faith in God." — Mark 11:22

The writer to the Hebrews says, "Without faith, it is impossible to please Him, for he who comes to God must believe that He is, and that He is a rewarder of those who diligently seek Him" (Heb. 11:6).

It follows then that without this faith, it is impossible to earn the Divine attestation: "This is My beloved Son, in whom I am well *pleased*" (Matt. 3:17, emphasis mine), or "Well done, good and faithful servant" (Matt. 25:21).

Faith, in the sense of the above text, is not an attribute of God, but His essential nature. Therefore, only those who are partakers of God's divine nature are possessors of it. Moreover, it is increased as *Christ* (who is God's nature) is formed in me.

Lord, increase my faith. I believe, help my unbelief.

"And the common people heard Him gladly."
— Mark 12:37

These were the people who recognized and enjoyed the ministry of the Lord Jesus. A little further down in this same chapter, the Lord admonishes and denounces the Scribes and Pharisees, for though they appeared to be religious or godly, they were absolute hypocrites. The common people were those who not only recognized their need for teaching and healing, but also realized that the Lord Jesus could meet that need. Therefore, He says, "I did not come to call the righteous, but sinners, to repentance" (Matt. 9:13).

Surely, it is to the common people that the Lord would have me go. If He could mix with sinners and publicans, surely it is for me to do likewise.

Embolden me Lord, as I seek to share
Your Word to those whose path I cross in
my daily comings and goings.

"For it is not you who speak, but the Holy Spirit."
— *Mark 13:11*

What a promise to claim before setting forth
to preach the Gospel! It is the ministry of the
Holy Spirit to present and reveal Christ. So
that if it is He that speaks through me today,
how fruitful will the ministry be!

The essentials are: Cleansing, Emptying,
Filling with the Holy Spirit, Absolute
Reliance upon Him for speaking, praying, and
all service. Such reliance is vitally important if
I am to be genuine when I preach Christ.

Then empty me, Lord. Cleanse me by Your precious blood.
Now fill with me the Holy Spirit. I take the fullness,
and thank You. Control me in all I do and say,
that You might be glorified today. Amen.

"She has done a good work for Me." — Mark 14:6

What a blessed commendation! Such was given in response to the outpouring of the sweet and precious spikenard – a token of true heart love.

The Lord called it a "good work." Good because it was seen by the Lord from the spiritual side. Man, like those who murmured saying, "Why this waste?" (v. 4), looks at the outward appearance, but God looks at the heart. And as He looked, He saw that it was the true expression of unadulterated love. God looked at creation and said it was "very good." The Lord looked at this woman's heart and saw that His work in her heart was good.

When You look at my heart, Lord,
I pray You find this same quality of love.

"He answered nothing." — Mark 15:3

Surely, this is where grace in all its divine splendor shines forth!

He who called the world into existence by the utterance of a word, He who upholds the worlds by the word of His power, He who could have asked His Father for more than twelve legions of angels to come to His aid – this One, my blessed Lord, stood in that judgment hall, "bearing shame and scoffing rude"[5] and "answered nothing" (v. 3).

Oh, matchless grace, that Jesus there alone
On Calv'ry's cross for sinners should atone:
To such a Friend, a Saviour and a King
Our lives for service we will gladly bring.[6]

"The Lord working with them." – Mark 16:20

This is the promise to all true disciples. And what an honor! The Lord working with *me*! How absolutely incredible! Yet it is true – blessed be His Holy Name.

Yes, He has promised to be with me right to the end of the age. He has said, "I will never leave you nor forsake you" (Heb. 13:5). "My presence will go with you" (Ex. 33:14).

One of the obvious proofs of His presence and working power is the confirmation of His Word, with signs following. How clearly these signs shone in the days of the early apostles. Thousands were being added to the church daily.

Lord, give me a true evidence that You
are working with or through me, or else,
"do not bring [me] up from here" (Ex. 33:15).

*"He will turn many of the children of Israel
to the Lord their God."* — Luke 1:16

What a blessed mission for a Son of Adam!
Truly, "How beautiful are the feet of those
who preach the gospel of peace, who bring
glad tidings of good things!" (Rom. 10:15).

Because of such a mission, John the Baptist
was to be "great in the sight of the Lord" (Luke
1:15). As to John himself, he was to touch no
strong drink and he was to be filled with the
Spirit from his very birth.

The application of these few thoughts is
obvious. The Lord has said, "He that wins
souls is wise" (Prov. 11:30), that is, great in His
sight. But in order to be qualified to "turn
many to righteousness" (Daniel 12:3), the
message to be worked out in practical
experience is "Do not be drunk with wine, in
which is dissipation; but be filled *with the
Spirit*" (Eph. 5:18, emphasis mine).

*May I be filled with Your spirit, Lord,
in order to bear witness to Your grace and truth.*

EVENING READING: LUKE 2

"[They] *supposing Him to have been*
in the company . . ." — Luke 2:44

Herein is seen the folly of supposition.
Concerning things that are spiritual, such
supposition is fatal.

From a parental point of view, it was folly
on the part of Joseph and Mary to merely
suppose that the Lord Jesus was in the
company. No wonder it meant their sorrowing
for Him later.

But from a spiritual point of view, it was even
worse. To merely *suppose* that Christ is in the
company is spiritual defeat and sorrow. Three
days His parents lost Him – three days the
disciples lost Him. The third day He arose.

*O then, not to suppose, but to know Him and
the power of His Resurrection. Amen.*

*"The word of God came unto John . . .
in the wilderness."* — Luke 3:2

In Luke 1:80, it is recorded of John that he was
"in the deserts till the day of his manifestation
to Israel."

It is very obvious that the desert or the
wilderness were God's training school for this
coming Man of God. He had to learn of God
in private before preaching in public.

The wilderness speaks of the place of
retirement, rest, and quiet. It is only in such a
place that God can teach the more intimate
and secret revelations of His will. It is very
interesting and important to note, the number
of times the Lord Jesus sought the quiet and
retirement of the wilderness during his
ministry (Luke 5:16). It is the place where the
Word of God becomes the real weapon for the
battle of preaching.

*Lord, make my times with You a desert experience
full of rest and revelation from You.*

"I must preach." — Luke 4:43

These were the words of the perfect preacher, the Lord Jesus Christ. His very heart burned with a holy passion for souls. "I must preach," it was imperative. His great love compelled Him. His holy ministry was characterized by His devotedness to His ministry. He was to seek and to save. Therefore:

- He *must* be about His Father's business (Luke 2:49).
- He *must* preach (Luke 4:43).
- He *must* go through Samaria (John 4:4).
- He *must* be lifted up (John 12:32).

The apostle Paul burned with the same spiritual zeal. He therefore could say, "Necessity is laid upon me; yes, woe is me if I do not preach the gospel!" (1 Cor. 9:16). And, "Brethren, my heart's desire and prayer to God for Israel is that they might be saved" (Rom. 10:1).

Create this passion within my soul, O Lord.

"Launch out into the deep." — Luke 5:4

Here is a message to my heart. The Lord bids me "launch out into the deep." There is too much shallow fishing these days. He calls for deepwater fishing. It is true that deepwater fishing requires far more effort, skill, resource, and courage. And because of this, the Devil would gladly discourage me. But the Lord says, "Do not be afraid. From now on you will catch men" (Luke 5:10).

In essence, my Savior is saying to me, "Fear not about the extra effort. My strength is sufficient for you. Fear not about the needed skill. Have I not promised to make you a fisher of men? Fear not about resources; I am able to supply all your need. Fear not, take courage, for though you might begin to sink, My hand will be outstretched to save; though the Storm should violently blow, I shall still it; though the angry waves beat into the ship, fear not. I shall speak peace to them and there shall be a calm. But launch out!"

*I shall launch out, Lord, knowing that You
are sufficient to supply and strong to save!*

"But if you love those who love you, what credit is that
to you? For even sinners love those who love them."
— Luke 6:32

For the perfect example of the principle
enshrined in this verse read John 3:16; 14:23;
Romans 5:18; Galatians 2:20; 1 John 4:10.

God loved a world that was at enmity with Him.
When He sent His beloved Son, the world did
not receive Him; even "His own did not
receive Him. (John 1:11). God *commended His
love toward us* (as individuals), "in that while
we were still sinners, Christ died for us" (Rom.
5:8). So the apostle John says, "In this is love,
not that we loved God, but that He loved us"
(1 John 4:10). Notice also Galatians 2:20.
God also has a special love for His own children.
"Behold what manner of love the Father has
bestowed on us, that we should be called
children of God!" (1 John 3:1). God's children,
though, are called to obey Him, and in so
doing they demonstrate their love. God loves
the unlovely and unloving, and so must I.

*Help me to have compassion for and embrace
those who do not love me, for Your Name's sake. Amen.*

"Go and tell John the things you have seen and heard:
that the blind see, the lame walk, the lepers are cleansed,
the deaf hear, the dead are raised, the poor have
the gospel preached to them."
— Luke 7:22

John had just sent two disciples to Jesus to inquire whether He was the Christ (the sent One) or not. In reply to the inquiry, the Lord Jesus gave evidence of His Messiahship. "Go," said He, "and tell John the things you have seen and heard."

The blind see. "To open their eyes" (spiritually; Acts 26:18). Christ brought revelation. *The lame walk.* Emancipation. *The lepers are cleansed.* Spiritual cleansing and forgiveness. *The deaf hear.* The hearing of faith (Rom. 10:17). *The dead are raised.* Life. "He is not the God of the dead but of the living" (Luke 20:38). "I have come," said the Savior, "that they may have life" (John 10:10). *The Gospel is preached.* In the Gospel is comprehended *all.* "It is the power of God to salvation for everyone who believes" (Rom. 1:16).

Thank You, Father, for not just asking us to believe
but showing us why we can believe.

EVENING READING: LUKE 8

"Then they went out to see what had happened,
and came to Jesus, and found the man."
— Luke 8:35

A wonderful miracle had been performed. A man, who was more of a beast than a human being, had been completely changed. Though no man could bind him (not even with chains) or tame him, Christ had delivered him. The people in the surrounding district heard of it, and they came out to see what was done. What did they see? They saw Jesus. To whom did they come? They came to Jesus. In doing so, they found the man sitting at the feet of Jesus, clothed and in his right mind.

If I am to see what You can do and will do,
I must come to You.

"Jesus said to him, 'Do not forbid him, for he who is not against us is on our side.'" — Luke 9:50

John had seen one casting out devils in the name of the Lord Jesus, and just because he did not recognize this man to be a disciple (or one who followed with the twelve), he forbade him. John said distinctly, "Because he does not follow with *us*" (Luke 9:48, emphasis mine). He did not seem to realize that a person could be a sincere follower of the Lord Jesus, without necessarily being outwardly associated with the disciples.

The Lord Jesus, however, said, "Do not forbid him, for he who is not against us is on our side." He could look at the heart, while John merely looked at the outward appearance. The Lord was satisfied; John was not. Jesus did not condemn the man, but John did. O, how simple it is to condemn fellow Christians just because they do not follow us.

Lord, help me to be able to comprehend with all saints, what is the length and breadth of Your love.

"*Many prophets and kings have desired to see what you see, and have not seen it, and to hear what you hear, and have not heard it.*" — Luke 10:24

O Lord, I do bow in deep heart gratitude, when I consider Your grace which has made me a "seer" and a "hearer" of things, which prophets and kings have desired to look into but have failed.

I adore and worship You for the fact that You have in infinite love, revealed Your Father to me, and that now through the knowledge of God, I possess eternal life.

I do pray, Lord, that You would be pleased to continue to reveal the glories of the Father, as I read and meditate upon Your Word. For the sake of Your name and glory.

Amen.

"The lamp of the body is the eye. Therefore, when your eye is good, your whole body also is full of light. But when your eye is bad, your body also is full of darkness." — Luke 11:34

The eye cannot contain light in itself; it reflects light from the source of light. If therefore the body is to be full of light, the eyes must be focused on the true source of light, even the Lord Jesus. Hence, the apostle says, "Looking unto Jesus" (Heb. 12:2).

Fellowship is only maintained as I walk in the light even as my Lord is in the light. How necessary it is then, that my eyes be fixed on Him.

Turn your eyes upon Jesus,
Look full in His wonderful face,
And the things of earth will grow strangely dim,
In the light of His glory and grace.[7]

EVENING READING: LUKE 12

*"Do not seek what you should eat or what you should
drink, nor have an anxious mind."*
— Luke 12:29

What a message for today! When men and
nations in the world are very nearly beside
themselves with anxiety.

"Do not seek," said the Lord, "what you should
eat or what you should drink, nor have an
anxious mind." And previously, "Consider the
ravens, they neither sow nor reap . . . and God
feeds them. . . . Consider the lilies, how they
grow: they neither toil nor spin; and yet I say
to you, even Solomon in all his glory was not
arrayed like one of these. If then God so
clothes the grass . . . how much more will He
clothe you" (Luke 12:24-28)?

To live in anxiousness is a definite sin. For
it is rank faithlessness and what is not of faith
is sin.

*Father, give me the faith of the raven and lily.
Amen.*

"Strive to enter through the narrow gate."
— Luke 13:24

The word "strive" means "agonize" or "contend."

The gate to eternal life is not one into which men simply drift. On the contrary, no one will ever gain entrance without personally striving or agonizing. The picture presented by the word "agonize" is that of a woman in travail. She agonizes before new life is brought into the world. In like manner, it is only he who travails in soul agony who enters that narrow gate to life everlasting. It requires personal effort and striving to be a possessor of new life.

Moreover, striving does not end until the ultimate goal is reached. It is true that He gives grace and His yoke is easy, but it means real contending for the faith right to the end.

*"May I contend for the faith
and strive according to Your working in me."*
— Colossians 1:29

"Salt is good." — Luke 14:34

It *preserves.* This is a well known fact. Spiritualized, it is also true that the salt of the grace of Christ preserves one's life from impurity.

It *seasons.* Salt is used for seasoning. How true this is of the spiritual salt of grace. How it seasons life, making it sweet and acceptable before God and man.

It *is potent.* Good salt is very potent. It permeates all with which it comes into contact. Such should be spiritual salt in the Christian life. It should affect all with whom it comes into contact.

However, it is possible for salt to lose its savor.

Lord, grant that this shall not be my experience.

"Then all the tax collectors and the sinners
drew near to Him to hear Him." — Luke 15:1

What a grand fact!

It is interesting to note how the ministry of the Lord primarily attracted the publicans and sinners. It is recorded: "The common people heard Him gladly" (Mark 12:37). He said, "I did not come to call the righteous, but sinners, to repentance" (Matt. 9:13). "The Son of Man has come to seek and to save that which was lost" (Luke 19:10). Paul testifies: "Christ Jesus came into the world to save sinners, of whom I am chief" (1 Tim. 1:15). In the light of these few verses, it is obvious that the Lord's ministry not only attracted sinners but also was primarily for them. How important to have His message and mission today!

O, that Your ministry, Lord, through me
would draw the publicans and sinners to Yourself.

"He who is faithful in what is least
is faithful also in much." — Luke 16:10

What God looks for in His servants is not primarily success, but faithfulness. In the parable of the talents, the Master is recorded as saying: "Well done, good and faithful servant" (Matt. 25:21), and not, "Well done, good and successful servant."

The essence of faithfulness is exhibited in that which is least. Anyone is faithful, or can be so, in great matters. But he that can be faithful in the small things is he who is faithful.

In any case, God can use our faithfulness in the small things for His greater purpose and glory.

Lord, make me faithful to You.

"If your brother sins against you, rebuke him;
and if he repents, forgive him." – Luke 17:3

The Lord leaves no excuse for compromise in
His teaching. Here He lays down a principle:
rebuking sin and forgiving the repentant.

Rebuking Sin. He who does not rebuke sin is
a compromiser with sin. The Lord Jesus
exposed and rebuked sin continually during
His ministry. He did not even spare His own
disciples. Jesus said to Peter, "Get behind me,
Satan [Peter]" (Matt. 16:23). The apostle Paul,
in writing to the young man Timothy,
exhorted him thus: "Those who are sinning
rebuke in the presence of all, that the rest also
may fear" (1 Tim. 5:20).

Forgiving the Repentant. This is the outward or
public forgiveness. That is to say, after
rebuking a brother before the Lord, he should
be forgiven; but the public expression of this
must follow the trespasser's outward
repentance. "Forgiving one another, just as
God in Christ forgave you" (Eph. 4:32).

Lord, give me the courage to rebuke sin
and the love to forgive the sinner.

"See, we have left all and followed You."
— Luke 18:28

Peter must have had a poor conception of his Lord when he said these words. No doubt, the words were true enough, humanly speaking. But when compared to the preciousness of the blessed Lord, such words should never have been uttered. "We have left *all*." What was the *all* anyway, when compared with "all the spiritual blessings . . . in Christ" (Eph. 1:3, KJV)? He obviously had not risen to the experience of the apostle Paul when he could say: "I count *all* things . . . as rubbish, that I may gain Christ" (Phil. 3:8). Or again, "My God shall supply *all* your need" (Phil. 4:19).

O Lord, grant that I shall never consider
that I have given anything up for You.
For You have become ALL the world to me.

"The Lord has need of him." – Luke 19:34

The ass or even the colt was a beast of burden. It could carry valuable or valueless burdens. But on this particular occasion, the animal was required for the purpose of bearing a very important burden – *the Lord had need of him.* The Lord still requires beasts of burden – those upon whom He can lay important burdens. He says, "Take my yoke upon you" (Matt. 11:29), carry my burden.

Notice also how the answer of the disciples (or rather the Lord through His disciples) silenced those who tried to question their taking the colt. When the errand is a divinely controlled one, there is no stopping it. "If God is for us, who can be against us?" (Rom. 8:31).

Lord, "Here am I, send me." (Isaiah 6:8)

"Those who are counted worthy to attain that age,
and the resurrection from the dead." — Luke 20:35

"Counted worthy" – what a blessed expression! Especially when I consider on what grounds I shall be counted worthy to obtain that world and the resurrection.

By nature, there is "none who does good" (Rom. 3:12). "All have sinned" (Rom. 3:23). In flesh, "nothing good dwells" (Rom. 7:18). But on the grounds of the atoning work and person of the Lord Jesus, I have been "accepted in the Beloved" (Eph. 1:6), not having my own righteousness, but the righteousness which is of Christ. Therefore, I have been counted worthy to be a partaker of the inheritance in Light, "to attain that age, and the resurrection from the dead."

I am a sinner and yet He counts me worthy.
Blessed be His Name!

*"Watch therefore, and pray always that you
may be counted worthy." – Luke 21:36*

The *worthiness* of this verse is somewhat
different from the worthiness of Luke 20:35.
Here, the conditions are stated as being first,
watchful, then second, prayerful.

Watchful. This is consistent vigilance – the
vigilance of the watchman on the lookout,
who is ready to give the alarm or warning
immediately if the enemy is sighted. He who
sleeps will never be counted worthy.

Prayerful. Notice it says, "Pray always." In other
words, fulfilling such injunctions as "Pray
without ceasing" (1 Thess. 5:17), "Men always
ought to pray and not lose heart" (Luke 18:1),
and "Praying always with all prayer and
supplication" (Eph. 6:18).

Watching is sighting the enemy. Praying is
fighting the enemy. Only then will I be
accounted worthy.

> *Help me to watch and pray,*
> *And still on Thee rely,*
> *O let me not my trust betray,*
> *But press to realms on high.*[8]

"And He said to them, 'When I sent you without money
bag . . . did you lack anything?' So they said, 'Nothing.'"
— Luke 22:35

Loving Father, I do thank You for the fact that I can
faithfully and gratefully say with the disciples of old
– "I have lacked NOTHING."

I thank You that You have supplied all MY
NEEDS, despite the fact that You sent me forth
without purse. Indeed, Father, You have done far
exceeding abundantly above what I could have
asked or thought. Blessed be Your Holy Name
forever.

I thank You most of all, however, for the
Unspeakable Gift, the Lord Jesus Christ, for all that
He is and will ever be to me; for all that has come
and will yet come to me through Him; I bow in
heartfelt thankfulness.

Amen.

"I find no fault in this Man." — Luke 23:4

What an amazing testimony was this!

Pilate was only an unconverted Gentile, yet he had to say, "I find no fault in this Man."

The Lord Jesus Himself had only recently said, "Which of you convicts Me of sin?" (John 8:46). He said that even the Devil had no occasion against Him.

Yes, His life was one of spotless purity and goodness – an example to man and angels. Even the Father could say, "This is My beloved Son, in whom I am well pleased" (Matt. 3:17).

Blessed Lord, enable me by Your power to live
the faultless life, that Your Name may be glorified.

*"Their eyes were restrained, so that
they did not know Him." — Luke 24:16*

Spiritual Restriction. "Their eyes were
restrained" (v. 16). They were not able to see.
Their vision was limited or restricted by
unbelief. The fruits of such spiritual restriction
are sorrow (v. 17) and perplexity (v. 22).

Spiritual Revelation. "He expounded to them in
all the Scriptures the things concerning
Himself" (v. 27). After rebuking unbelief, this
One opened the Scriptures to the two
disciples. The weapon for unbelief is the Word
of God. When unbelief is dealt with through
opening of the Scriptures (see Heb. 4:12),
there is a real *heart experience* – the love of God
shed abroad in the heart by the Holy Spirit.

Spiritual Recognition. "Their eyes were opened
and they knew Him" (v. 31). "They knew
Him." This is the greatest height of spiritual
existence. Paul aspired to it – "That I might
know Him and the power of His resurrection"
(Phil. 3:10).

*I am grateful, Lord, for Your living Word that restores my
vision and faith, and allows me to know You.*

*"Looking at Jesus as He walked, he said,
'Behold the Lamb of God!'"* – John 1:36

Here in verse 36, it is not "The Lamb of God
who takes away the sin of the world" (v. 29),
but just "The Lamb of God." This verse
portrays a slightly different aspect of Christ to
the truth of verse 29. Again, here it is the
"Lamb." As He walked, the Lamb speaks of:

Absolute Submission. If ever there was a
submissive creature, the lamb certainly stands
out as the supreme example. Submission to
the will of God.

Absolute Selflessness. The lamb is the picture of
absolute humility and selflessness. Such was
the character of the Lord Jesus (see Matt.
11:28; Phil. 2).

Absolute Separation. The parted hoof of the
lamb pictures and speaks of separation. The
path of the Lord Jesus was one of separation
– "Separate from sinners" (Heb. 7:26).

Behold the Lamb of God!

"Zeal for Your house has eaten Me up." — John 2:17

The Lord Jesus is the perfect example in all departments of life. With that fact in view, it is instructive to notice His perfect behavior in reverence for and interest in the House of God.

In light of the above verse, it would seem that His holy zeal burned at its highest when the House of God was the object of particular interest. Of course, His Holy zeal always burned at its highest. But it is the phrase "Eat me up," that makes one use comparative language. John Nelson Darby translates it "Devours me."[9] What a zeal He had for the interests and work of God's House.

Father, give me a zeal for Your house
like Your blessed Son's. Amen.

"God does not give the Spirit by measure." – John 3:34

It is quite obvious that the reference here is to the Lord Jesus Christ. But nevertheless, this is God's principle – He never gives by measure. He *so* loved that He gave His only begotten Son. He *did not spare* His Son. If He did not spare, it follows that He does not give by measure. For in giving His Son, through Him He now freely gives me all things (not by measure!).

The question of the "measure," however, is governed by the life of the believer. Paul speaks of Christians who were not able to receive the meat of the Word because of carnality. The human vessel can only be filled in so far as it is emptied. The Lord was "The Empty One" for He emptied Himself (See Phil. 2). Therefore, the Spirit was given to Him without measure.

Lord, I empty myself entirely that I may be filled to overflowing with Your Holy Spirit.

"The man believed the word." – John 4:50

Here is certainly a good example of expectant faith. The Lord simply said to him, "Your son lives" (v. 51) and he believed the Word. The result was that his son was healed.

This is the source of real spiritual blessing – namely, believing and claiming the promises of God. There must be *expectant* faith, however. James says, "Let not that man [who wavers in the prayer of faith] suppose that he will receive anything from the Lord" (James 1:7). Expectant faith is the key to the verse which says, "Ask, and you will receive" (John 16:24).

O Lord help me, I pray, to believe Your Word
even as this man did. Amen.

"I do not receive honor from men." — John 5:41

The Lord Jesus spoke these words to men who were bent on slaying Him. They were the Pharisees and Scribes who honored one another rather than God (v. 44). Even when they did appear to honor God, it was only mere lip-service; their hearts were far from Him. These men were hypocrites and lived criticizing others. If Christ therefore received honor from such, surely it would appear that He were condoning their hypocrisy and evil. On the other hand, the statement of the Lord Jesus in the above verse condemned rather than condoned the evil works of these Pharisees.

If my blessed Lord did not receive honor from men, how will I ever expect to receive honor from those who live to criticize?

Give me, O Lord, the Spirit of Grace.

Evening Reading: John 6

"It is I; do not be afraid." — John 6:20

What grand words! How they strengthen, cheer, and comfort the heart. It is true that these words were uttered at a dark moment in the experience of the disciples, but these same words are still the words of the Lord Jesus, and therefore continue to carry with them their ancient power.

He says, "It is I, do not be afraid." There is no need to fear when He is near. He is the perfect Love which casts out fear. Moreover, He has said, "I will never leave you nor forsake you" (Heb. 13:5), and with the Hebrew writer, I reply "The LORD is my helper; I will not fear. What man can do to me?" (Heb. 13:6). "It is I" (John 6:20) – "If God is for [me], who can be against [me]?" (Rom. 8:31).

Lord, in these uncertain times,
Your Word brings comfort and peace.

"If anyone thirsts, let him come to Me and drink."
— John 7:37

There are three steps in this verse. Each one is as important as the other, and all lead to true satisfaction in Christ.

Rapacity – a greedy desire or craving for the Living Water. "If anyone thirsts." There must be this earnest desire if the soul is to be satisfied, for the Word says, "Blessed are those who hunger and thirst for righteousness, for they shall be filled" (Matt 5:6).

Request – "Let him come to Me." This is request, for it includes the two parties: *he* who thirsts coming to the *One* who satisfies. That coming is the request of the soul.

Reception – "Drink." Here is the personal deliberate reception of the gift of satisfying water. "To drink" implies the receiving into oneself.

Satisfy my soul now, O Lord,
until I overflow with Your blessing.

"The truth shall make you free." — John 8:32

It is interesting to note the working powers of the Word of God or Truth as revealed in this Gospel. Here are just a few:

Its *Liberating power.* "The truth shall make you free." The Word of God is that which snaps all chains of bondage.

Its *Pruning power.* "You are already clean [pruned] because of the word which I have spoken to you" (John 15:3). This is pruning for greater fruitfulness.

Its *Sanctifying power.* "Sanctify them by Your truth. Your word is truth" (John 17:17). Herein lies the secret of a sanctified life.

Its *Rejoicing power.* "If you know these things, blessed are you if you do them" (John 13:17). The keeping of His commandments has a special reward of happiness for the obedient believer.

Thank You, Lord, for the liberating power of Your Word.
May Your Word have its way in my life.

"I must work the works of Him who sent Me while it is day." — John 9:4

The true principle of all real service for God underlies this statement of the Lord Jesus. And since He was the perfect Servant when upon this earth, He made this principle the basis of His loyal service to God.

The Obligation of True Service. The Lord Jesus said, "I *must* work." The obligation of loving and loyal service to His Father compelled Him to work. Yes, right from the beginning (remember the temple when He was twelve years old?) to the end.

The Occupation of True Service. There is only one great occupation in true service — it is doing God's will. I must work the "works of Him." "My food is to do the will of Him who sent Me," said the Savior (John 4:34).

The Opportunity of True Service. "While it is day." Now is the acceptable time . . . "Time is short" (1 Cor. 7:29).

I can do nothing else but serve You, Lord, all of my days,
For it is a privilege and an honor — yes, even my duty!

"John performed no sign, but all the things that John spoke about this Man were true." — John 10:41

What a testimony to covet! In the light of this one verse, it is clear that John the Baptist was not known:

By *the Miracles*. That which can be seen with the natural eye or superhuman outward manifestations.

By *the Supremacy of Self*. For he spoke of another, but he was known by his testimony concerning the Lord Jesus.

Notice, "All the things that John spoke about this Man were true." He "shunned not to declare . . . the *whole* counsel of God (Acts 20:27, emphasis mine). He was a true and faithful witness.

May I be known only by what I have to say concerning You, O Lord. Amen.

"Lazarus sleeps." — John 11:11

Jesus Christ, the Son of the living God, was and is the only One to make such a statement. In His presence, death is as sleep. Hence, He could say, "Lazarus sleeps."

A little farther down this chapter, the Lord Jesus says these words: "I am the resurrection and the life" (v. 25). What is death in the light of this pregnant statement? No wonder the apostle could challenge the king of terror, saying, "O Death, where is your sting? O Hades, where is your victory?" (1 Cor. 15:55).

In the light of this whole chapter, death appears to be the means through which God manifests His glory. It was so on this particular occasion. Christ's death was the means through which God was glorified (13:23-28). Death to self is the only basis on which Christ will be glorified in me.

Daily let me die to self so that You may be glorified.
Amen.

"Mary took a pound of very costly oil of spikenard,
[and] anointed the feet of Jesus." — John 12:3

This act of Mary expresses three things:

Her Faith. Faith had revealed to her that Jesus
was none other than the Lamb of God who
would take away the sin of the world. Thus,
she took the pound of oil, breaking it upon
Him in anticipation of His atoning death.

Her Hope. Hope had carried her beyond death
and the grave. Had she thought that Christ
would not rise, she would have kept the oil
until the burying for embalming.

Her Love. Above her faith and hope shines
forth her love in this act. For in that expensive
gift was expressed her unstinted, unreserved
love. Love is only measured by the sacrificial
gift; and the breaking of the vessel of
spikenard upon Him meant the sacrifice of
her all. No wonder the room was filled!

O, that my life would be as Mary's oil —
a sacrificial, unreserved gift to my Lord.

"[Jesus] rose from supper and laid aside His garments,
took a towel and girded Himself." — John 13:4

In this picture is presented supreme humility.
O to grasp the same spirit, that my life may be
characterized with the humility of my blessed
Lord.

He *rose from Supper.* Here was the deliberate
and intentional advance for the expression of
humility. It is true that He was incarnate
humility, but it is also true that He
deliberately came to express it.

He *laid aside His garments.* He emptied Himself
of all His glory. He who was rich became poor.

He *took a towel and girded Himself.* He took
upon Him the form of a servant. Girding is
essentially the sign of service. He could say,
"I am among you as the One who serves"
(Luke 22:27).

Teach me humility, O Lord.

"If it were not so, I would have told you." — John 14:2

Personally, this is a very wonderful thought. Christ says, "If all the things about which I have been talking were not so, I would have told you." Of course, this primary application is in connection with the few preceding words concerning the Father's house. And what a certain seal this was and is to the reality of a home in heaven for those who are His. But I like to apply the above verse to more than just the preceding few words. I like to take the *whole revelation* of Christ as recorded, and add, "Were this revelation not so, He would have told me." This precious thought seems to seal home to my own heart the essential truth of all He has said in His Word, for were it not so, He would have told me.

Your Word stands as Truth, Lord. Amen.

"By this My Father is glorified, that you bear much fruit;
so you will be My disciples." — John 15:8

The fruit in Chapter 15 of John is the fruit of *character* — namely, "love, joy, peace, longsuffering, kindness, goodness, faithfulness, gentleness, self-control" (Gal. 5:22-23). The production of these fruits, or better *this* fruit, is firstly, glorifying to God, and secondly, the expression of true discipleship.

These two great things were the supreme objects of Christ's life upon this earth. He lived and died to glorify the Father. He lived and died as the devoted loyal Bondslave of God.

These two objects can never be achieved without an unbroken fellowship and union with Christ (abiding). This is maintained through constant cleansing by the abiding Word and filling of the Spirit.

Cleanse me and fill me, Lord.
Produce in me Your sweet fruit of character. Amen.

"Whoever kills you will think that he offers God service."
— John 16:2

Here is certainly a sad state of spiritual affairs.
There is coming a time, and in fact in some
places it has already come, when the
departure from truth shall be such that men
who will not accept the real Truth will
persecute and kill the very servants of God.
Of course, this primarily applies to the time
when the abomination of desolation, spoken
of by Daniel and our Lord, will be set up in
the temple at Jerusalem, and the great
tribulation shall take place. But even now,
it is possible to be so misunderstood by those
who profess to bear the truth, as to provoke
hatred and persecution.

Enable me to stand for You, whatever the odds.
Amen.

Morning Reading: John 17

"These are in the world . . . They are not of the world . . .
I also have sent them into the world. . . . That the world
may believe that You sent me." — John 17:11, 16, 18, 21

"These are in the world" (v. 11). This is the
believer's *presence* in the world. It is the
sphere into which every man is born. It is the place
in which he has to live. If he is to be kept from
evil, he must seek the necessary power
through the name of God.

"They are not of the world" (v. 16). This is the
believer's *position* in the world. He is not of it,
so must live entirely independently of it.

"I also have sent them into the world" (v. 18). This
is the believer's *purpose* in the world. As Christ
was sent with and for a purpose, even so is the
believer sent, "That the world may believe . . ."
(v. 21).

I do pray for power and grace to live in relation to the
world as You have taught me here in Your Word. Amen.

"Jesus therefore, knowing all things that would
come upon Him, went forward and said to them,
'Whom are you seeking?'" — John 18:4

What grace is this! What love! "Greater love
has no one than this, than to lay down one's
life for his friends" (John 15:13). But this Man
handed himself over to His enemies, not His
friends. They had come with lanterns and
torches and weapons – they were His
enemies.

It was night when this greatest of incidents
took place. Judas knew that the Lord Jesus
resorted to the garden, but probably could not
distinguish Him right away in the dim light
of the torches and lanterns. But the blessed
Master, with His face set to do His Father's
will, never flinched, but walked out to meet
His enemies, saying, "I am He" (John 18:5).

Lord, give me the love that knows no fear
– the perfect Love.

"They took Jesus and led Him away." — John 19:16

Isaiah prophesies the same matchless grace of the Lord Jesus when he writes, "He was led as a lamb to the slaughter, and as a sheep before its shearers is silent, so He opened not His mouth" (Isa. 53:7).

Peter also says, "When He was reviled, did not revile in return; when He suffered, He did not threaten, but committed Himself to Him who judges righteously" (1 Pet. 2:23). A little before this verse are the words, "For to this you were called, because Christ also suffered for us, leaving us an example, that you should follow His steps" (1 Pet. 2:21).

"They took Jesus and led Him away" (John 19:16). What grace and humility are here manifest. He did not refuse to be led to the slaughter. Indeed, sacred love caused Him to be led in utter weakness that I might learn by His matchless example.

Lord, give me a measure of Your grace and humility when I face those who would persecute me.

"Jesus said to her, 'Mary!'" — John 20:16

Earlier in this Gospel, the Lord Jesus had given expression to these words, "He who enters by the door is the shepherd of the sheep. To him the doorkeeper opens, and the sheep hear his voice; and he calls his own sheep by name" (John 10:2, 3).

The Lord Jesus had just opened the door or way to the Father by His death and resurrection. He now stood before one of His puzzled and confused sheep. "Jesus said to her, 'Mary!'" He called His own sheep by name and the sheep knew His voice and followed Him.

It is grand to know that He has my name carved on the very palms of His hands.

May I ever be ready to hear my name called, and reply, "Master!"

MORNING READING: JOHN 21

"Cast the net on the right side of the boat." — John 21:6

Months and years have come and gone. Yes, gone forever. If I dare take stock of how I spend my time, what answers would or could I sincerely give to such questions as: "What progress have I made spiritually over the last year? What have I done to help extend the kingdom of God? How many souls have I won for Him? What fruit is apparent as a result of my ministry among God's people?" To such questions, I have to confess by way of answer that I have toiled all night and, generally speaking, have caught nothing.

Give me grace, Lord, to obey Your message to my heart —
"Cast the net on the right side of the boat." Amen.

"A witness with us of His resurrection." — Acts 1:22

It is very obvious from this verse and the surrounding verses that the fundamental qualification of a true witness is the knowledge of and the conscious responsibility to testify concerning the resurrection of the Lord Jesus Christ.

The resurrection of the Lord Jesus Christ is the foundation stone of all Christian doctrine. For, "If Christ is not risen, [our] faith is futile; [we] are still in [our] sins" (1 Cor. 15:17). The crucifixion of Jesus could be the martyrdom of a good man, but the resurrection of Jesus seals the death as being the atoning death of the Son of God.

How important then to be a true witness to the resurrection of my blessed Lord.

Lord, help me never to leave it out of my preaching.

Morning Reading: Acts 2

"For the promise is to you." — Acts 2:39

The promise of the filling of the Holy Spirit was not for the early apostles only. This very verse clearly indicates that the promise is for as many as the Lord our God shall call. If the promise to me is the same as to the early disciples, it follows that the power for witness that they had should also be my power.

The apostle Paul teaches later in his epistles that it is every Christian's responsibility to "Be filled with the Spirit" (Eph. 5:18). The Lord Jesus taught before He left this earth, "If you then, being evil, know how to give good gifts to your children, how much more will your heavenly Father give the Holy Spirit to those who ask Him" (Luke 11:13).

*Lord, teach me how to claim this promise rightly,
that I may be useful to You.*

"Power or godliness." — Acts 3:12

It is not without significance that Peter chooses these two words to describe the means through which the lame man was made whole. Notice that while Peter and John take no honor for the miracle, there is an obvious implication that the two essentials were power and godliness (or holiness, KJV). It is true that it was not their power and holiness, but it is also clear that power and holiness were necessary if God were to work. The apostle Paul in his introduction to the epistle of the Romans speaks of Christ thus, "Jesus Christ . . . declared to be the Son of God with power according to the Spirit of holiness" (Rom. 1:4-5). Christ is therefore the embodiment of these two great forces, and Christ was in and working through Peter and John.

Make clear to others, Lord, that it is Your power
and holiness that work through me.

"Whether it is right in the sight of God to listen to you more than to God, you judge." — Acts 4:19

These words were spoken by Peter and John to the rulers of the people and elders of Israel. They express the spirit of boldness and faithfulness which had stirred these poor fishermen, to "speak the things which [they had] seen and heard" (v. 20). The apostles themselves confess that they simply were compelled to speak for their Master, whatever the rulers and elders had to say.

Notice that their testimony was given "in the sight of God" (v. 19). Here was faithfulness. There were no ulterior motives or selfish desires. There was no attempt to please man. They were certain of the rightness of their testimony, for it was in the sight of God.

O Lord, inspire me with this zeal and holy boldness. Grant to Your servant, that with all boldness, I may speak Your Word.

*"They did not cease teaching and preaching
Jesus as the Christ."* — Acts 5:42

It is very instructive to notice the order of the
two words "teaching and preaching." The
disciples first taught the Lord Jesus Christ,
then preached Him. This is undoubtedly a
principle which should strictly be regarded
when working among people who do not
really know the message of the Gospel.

There is no doubt also in the order of the two
words "Jesus as the Christ." It is not "Christ
Jesus" here but "Jesus" (Savior) "the Christ"
(the Anointed or Sent One). In teaching and
preaching to the unsaved, it would seem from
this verse that the order should be Jesus as
Savior, then Christ as the Anointed One. This
is certainly true in experience.

*Let the example of Your disciples be my guide
when reaching the world for You, Lord.*

*"It is not desirable that we should leave the
word of God and serve tables." — Acts 6:2*

It was not for lack of humility that the
apostles said these words. It was rather that
the teaching and preaching of the Word of
God should not be hindered. This was
"desirable," or that which was right or proper.
Serving tables, though a duty important in
itself, was decided to be committed into the
hands of men who were spiritually qualified
to perform it.

The serving of tables consisted of the
pecuniary transactions of the Church. For
they had all things in common (Acts 4:32),
and this meant that there had to be those who
should distribute equally to all the material
needs of the Church. The lesson in the above
verse, however, is that, first, it is "desirable" to
hold the ministry of the Word in the place of
special importance; and yet not to neglect the
secondary duties in connection with the work
of God.

*The preaching of Your Word and the
ministry to Your people are both important works.
Help me to put them in proper priority.*

"Brethren and fathers, listen." — Acts 7:2

What has impressed me more than anything else in the reading of this chapter is Stephen's amazing knowledge of the now known "Old Testament." From the second verse until the fiftieth, he gives a most comprehensive and yet precise resumé of Old Testament history. How he must have studied the Scriptures! How acquainted he must have been with them, for a flow of language concerning his subject such as seen in these verses would have otherwise been impossible. The Holy Spirit only brings to remembrance such things as one has learned. Stephen must have been a real student of the Word, as was His Master.

Give me the power and needed grace, Lord,
to study to show myself approved unto God,
rightly dividing the Word of Truth.

"Give me this power also." – Acts 8:19

In verse 13, it is recorded of this Simon that he believed, was baptized, and continued with Phillip. From all external appearances, it would seem that he was a sacred man. But as Peter says in verse 22, Simon's heart was not right in the sight of God. This was manifested in the way he coveted the power of God for his own ulterior motives. "He offered them money" (v. 18). What an act of utter ingratitude! Is it any wonder Peter says, "Your money perish with you, because you thought that the gift of God could be purchased with money" (v. 20).

"Give me this power also." He did not desire it for God's glory. He merely wished to become as "someone great" (v. 9). He had not the love of the Father, but the love of the world. Notice that: "Simon saw . . . the laying on of the apostles' hands" – lust of the eyes (v. 18). "He offered them money, saying 'Give me'" – lust of the flesh (vv. 18-19). "Anyone on whom I lay hands may receive the Holy Spirit" – pride of life (v. 19).

Personal power is fleeting and for fleshly gain.
True power is from You and for Your Glory. Amen.

"Behold, he is praying." — Acts 9:11

It would seem that Saul spent three days, without sight, food, or drink (v. 9), yet praying all the while. What happened during those hours of prayer changed Saul into the great apostle Paul. Prostrate there before his Lord, Saul was emptied of all self-righteousness, pride, and arrogance, and filled with such a burning love for Christ that nothing could dim until he finished his course.

"Behold, he is praying." This was the attitude Ananias was to find him in – one of utter humility and self-abnegation. It was only when Paul had voluntarily and deliberately assumed this position and attitude that he could receive these three: (1) sight – what a spiritual sight Paul had; (2) the filling of the Spirit – Paul could write from experience saying, "Be filled with the Spirit" (Eph. 5:18); and, (3) strengthening – he finished the race (2 Tim. 4:7).

O, that I might have just a portion of
Paul's experience, Lord.

> *"God shows no partiality. . . . Whoever fears Him and works righteousness is accepted by Him."* — Acts 10:34-35

These verses contain the message that Peter preached to Cornelius and his house. When analyzed, it is very instructive to observe the whole Gospel in it, such as Christ commanded all disciples to teach.

God is no respecter of persons (v. 34). "There is no difference; for all have sinned" (Rom. 3:22-23), and yet all are entitled, through the acceptance in faith, to the "preaching peace through Jesus Christ – He is Lord of all" (Acts 10:36). *God has sent a Savior* (v. 38), whose life attested His divine mission and power. *The Savior, His death by crucifixion* (v. 39). *The Savior, His resurrection* (v. 40). God raised Him from the dead, thus setting His seal upon His life and death (atoning). *The Savior, the Forgiver of Sins to all who believe in Him* (v. 43). *The Sovereign work of the Holy Spirit* in the lives of all those who believe (v. 44). Then, "he commanded them to be baptized in the name of the Lord" (v. 48).

Lord, let the Gospel of the Lord Jesus Christ be preached clearly and completely.

EVENING READING: ACTS 11

"Peter explained it to them in order." — Acts 11:4

Here is the correct way to rehearse, declare, or teach the Truth. Paul says, when writing to the Corinthians, "Let all things be done decently and in order" (1 Cor. 14:40), and it applies here as well.

To expound Truth in or by order presupposes:

Study. No one can expound on a subject about which he knows nothing. In this case, Peter had seen the vision, had heard God speak, and had a good grasp of the Truth which God sought to impart.

Sequence. There is no order where there is no sequence. All thoughts or points should be marshaled in order of sequence.

System or Synthesis. The putting together of the message ready to be delivered.

*Lord, enable me to approach the preaching
and teaching of Your Word in a worthy manner.*

"He . . . did not know that what was done
by the angel was real." — Acts 12:9

It is no doubt significant that on the three
occasions Peter is recorded as sleeping, the
phrase "He did not know" also occurs:

Mark 9:6 – "He did not know what to say."
On this occasion, Peter and the other two
disciples were on the Mount of
Transfiguration. Luke says, "Peter and those
with him were heavy with sleep; and when
they were fully awake, they saw His glory"
(Luke 9:32). He slept but awakened to see the
Lord's Great Glory. *Mark 14:40 – "[Peter] did not
know what to answer Him."* Here again, Peter is
sleeping. This time it is in the Garden of
Gethsemane, and Peter witnesses the sorrow
of Christ. He slept but awakened to see the
Lord's Great Grace. *Acts 12:9 – "[Peter] did not
know that what was done by the angel was real."*
Peter is now in prison. He sleeps. The angel of
the Lord delivers him out of the hand of
Herod. He slept but awakened to see the
Lord's Great Goodness.

Lord, help me to be vigilant and not sluggish
so that I might witness Your great works.

"A man after My own heart, who will do all My will."
— Acts 13:22

With all David's failures, he was still a man after God's own heart. The reason for this lies in the fact that David's heart was always set on fulfilling all the will of God. Though he very often failed and on one occasion grievously sinned, the real attitude of the heart never changed. This is a fact that must be assumed, for God would otherwise never give utterance to such words as these. Moreover, while man looks on the outward appearance, God looks on the heart.

The heart here means the affections or desires. David had set his affections on things above. His desire was to fulfill all the will of God — "that good and acceptable and perfect will of God" (Rom. 12:2).

Enable me thus to live, O Lord.

"He did not leave Himself without witness." — Acts 14:17

What a message this is today! Men and women on every hand are talking about the fearful consequences that would result were Germany to conquer Britain. But while the preaching of the Gospel would no doubt be hindered, and while persecution and tragedy would abound, God would never leave Himself without a witness. He is the unchanging One. His years fail not. What He had done in the past, He will do in the present, indeed, and right through the coming eternity.

It is a grand thought, "Jesus Christ is the same yesterday, today, and forever" (Heb. 13:8).

Lord, do in and through Your humble servant, what You did in and through Paul and Barnabas. Be pleased to use me as Your witness while life shall last. Amen.

*"Men who have risked their lives for the name
of our Lord Jesus Christ."* — Acts 15:26

Another Scripture which comes to my mind
is "they did not love their lives to the death"
(Rev. 12:11).

What a compelling love for their Lord these
men must have had! Ready to be offered at
any moment; ready to suffer dangers,
persecutions, or poverty. Yes, they were men
that had risked their lives for the name of the
Lord Jesus Christ. Christ Himself said,
"Greater love has no one than this, than to lay
down one's life for his friends" (John 15:13). It
is the love that is ready for sacrifice, even if it
is the sacrifice of life.

*O Lord, give me this love for You,
that come what may, I may be faithful to You.*

"Lydia . . . the Lord opened her heart." — Acts 16:14

There are three steps to be observed in the experience of Lydia:

An Open Heart. Here was the gradual work of the Holy Spirit in the heart of this woman. Her heart, like the flower, had opened to receive the spiritual dew and she was saved.

An Open Confession. She was baptized. In this act of obedience to her Lord's command, she openly identified herself with her Master in His death, burial, and resurrection life.

An Open Home. "Faith without works is dead" (James 2:26). But Lydia said, "If you have judged me to be faithful to the Lord, come to my house and stay" (Acts 16:15). Here was living faith bearing true fruit. Here was true women's ministry begotten by true love to the Lord and His servants. Here was extravagant mercy!

Open my heart, enlarge it, Lord.

*"His spirit was provoked within him when he saw that
the city was given over to idols."* — Acts 17:16

Paul was a man who had a real passion for
souls. He could say in writing to the Romans,
"Brethren, my heart's desire and prayer for
Israel is that they may be saved" (Rom. 10:1).
He was ready to "become all things to all men,
that [he] might by all means save some"
(1 Cor. 9:22). A man who has a real love for the
Lord and a real passion for the souls of men is
a man whose spirit is provoked within him
when he sees men wallowing in sin and
ignorance. "His spirit was provoked" (Acts
17:16). It was the same provocation shown by
the Master when He saw the idols of cattle
and money brought into His House.

*Lord, give me this concern, I pray,
for Your Name's sake. Amen.*

"Do not be afraid, but speak, and do not keep silent;
for I am with you." — Acts 18:9-10

Is it any wonder Paul could say, "Woe is me if I do not preach the Gospel" (1 Cor. 9:16)?

This was the message that God gave to Moses. Moses, however, refused on the grounds of his incompetence. Though the Lord had promised to be with his mouth, Moses refused. The result was that the Lord gave the honor to his brother Aaron.

The contrast is seen in John the Baptist. He obeyed the Word of the Lord and fulfilled His mission to the praise of his Lord. John could say, "I am the voice" (John 1:23). He posed as nothing more than a voice.

The greatest example is seen in my blessed Lord, who never held His peace when it came to teaching and preaching the Word of God. He kept at His Father's business.

Lord, give me the grace to obey the message
You have given me. Amen.

"God worked unusual miracles by the hands of Paul."
— Acts 19:11

What a powerful man Paul became for God!
So surrendered was he that God could use
him "unusually." The King James Version
translates it "special" miracles. It is the greatest
honor possible to be used at all. But to be
unusually or specially used for God is the
privilege of only those who surrender
themselves to God for His service.

The character of the powers or miracles which
he performed was previously unheard of. Paul
had every reason to be puffed up, yet he could
say he was "less than the least of all the saints"
(Eph. 3:8), indeed the chief among sinners
(see 1 Tim. 1:15).

Lord, reveal to me the whole secret of this man's life
that I may be used for Your glory. Amen.

"I am innocent of the blood of all men." — Acts 20:26

"I always lived among you, serving the Lord with all humility" (vv. 18-19).

"I kept back nothing that was helpful" (v. 20).

"I have not shunned to declare to you the whole counsel of God" (v. 27).

"I testify to you . . . that I am innocent of the blood of all men" (v. 26).

"I did not cease to warn everyone night and day with tears" (v. 31).

"I have coveted no one's silver or gold or apparel. Yes, you yourselves know that these hands have provided for my necessities, and for those who were with me" (v. 33-34).

This was Paul's testimony before the brethren at Ephesus. He was to see their faces no more, but he left "innocent of the blood of all men." What a standard!

O Lord, give me the grace to aspire to this standard.

Evening Reading: Acts 21

"We knelt down on the shore and prayed. When we
had taken our leave of one another, we boarded the ship,
and they returned home." — Acts 21:5-6

How quick Paul is to publicly witness for God.
It is true that the prayer and the bidding of
farewell in this verse concerned the disciples
who came to the beach with him. But
nevertheless, there were undoubtedly many
of the ship's crew and strangers around who
witnessed this impressive scene.

Notice also that women and children had left
the city together with their husbands to bring
Paul and the disciples on their way. What love
and loyalty! What fellowship and interest.
And together they knelt down to pray before
bidding each other farewell. How beautiful!

O, that there might be more of this spirit
among Your people today, Lord.

"I am Jesus of Nazareth." — Acts 22:8

What grace is exhibited in these words! He who was God of very God, "King of kings and Lord of lords" (1 Tim. 6:15), chose not to call Himself by any other title than "Jesus of Nazareth" on this particular occasion. The answer for this is simply, yet amazingly, His Grace. Had the Lord desired to take the life of this blasphemer and persecutor, He could have righteously done so. But no, He "did not come to judge the world but to save the world" (John 12:47).

So in answer to Paul's or Saul's question, "Who are You, Lord?" Christ replied, "I am Jesus of Nazareth," the name of humility, the name by which His kinsmen and friends and enemies called Him! Jesus of Nazareth, the Carpenter's Son! Was it any wonder that Paul was convicted? The Savior of Nazareth – therefore your Savior, Paul – even though you have persecuted Me!

*"Amazing Grace! How sweet the sound
That saved a wretch like me!"*[10]

Evening Reading: Acts 23

"Paul's sister's son heard of their ambush." — Acts 23:16

Here is an example of how God preserves His own. The story is not only interesting, but also instructive from this point of view.

Here is a lad, of no importance most probably as far as the human side goes, but nevertheless, just as useful to God as the lad with the five loaves and fishes. With this instrument, God made a way of escape for His servant, when his position was otherwise hopeless.

"If God is for us, who can be against us?" (Rom. 8:31). Our God is able. He is a God with whom nothing is impossible.

Give me the faith of God, O Lord. Amen.

*"According to the Way which they call a sect,
so I worship the God of my fathers."* — Acts 24:14

It is interesting to note how many times the term "the Way," occurs in this book. It was an appellation that was given to all followers of the Lord Jesus Christ. Though given, no doubt, in disdain, it was nevertheless a very applicable designation. For all such believers were the followers of the One who said, "I am the way" (John 14:6).

It is also interesting that from the very beginning, unbelievers and those who, though religious, would not accept the teaching of Christ, called "The Way" a sect or a heresy! Is it any wonder that the Truth and the way of Christ are challenged and opposed today?

Note how boldly Paul asserts, "According to the Way, so I worship God" (Acts 24:14).

Lord, keep me true to the Way.

"If I am an offender, or have committed anything deserving of death, I do not object to dying." — Acts 25:11

How confidently Paul speaks. The reason for this simply lay in the fact that he had lived in all good conscience before God. His life was lived under the searching and holy light of God, hence he had nothing wrong to confess.

Is it any wonder that God could use him so mightily! O, *to know the secret of this man. Lord, give me the confidence of this man that I might be able to testify as he did.* Like his Lord, Paul in this verse was in effect saying, "Which of you convicts Me of sin?" (John 8:46).

Hear my prayer, O Lord. Amen.

"From the power of Satan to God." – Acts 26:18

In this verse is presented a five-fold ministry. The servant of the Lord should take note, for it comprehends the ground he should cover when preaching the Gospel:

Illumination. "To open their eyes" – This is effected by presenting truth in the power of the Holy Spirit. *Conversion.* "To turn them from darkness to light" – The servant of the Lord should lead the seeking soul at this stage, leading from the darkness of ignorance into the light of the truth. *Emancipation.* "From the power of Satan to God" – This is where the greatest battle in the salvation of a soul is fought. The weapons to be used are The Stand (the blood of the Lamb); The Sword (the Word of God); and The Sanction (the Name of the Lord Jesus Christ). *Remission of Sins.* "They may receive forgiveness of sins" – Here is the cross, where forgiveness of sins is to be found through the blood. *Sanctification.* "An inheritance among those who are sanctified by faith in Me" – With all the blessings that a holy life brings.

*Enable me to preach the whole of
Your Gospel, Lord, leaving nothing out.*

EVENING READING: ACTS 27

"I believe God." — Acts 27:25

This amazing statement of Paul's was no mere platitude. Neither was it said when circumstances around were particularly congenial. On the contrary, Paul gave utterance to these words when everything spoke of utter hopelessness, desperation, and despondency. Having not eaten for a fortnight, Paul was now faced, humanly speaking, with death – through sheer weakness, death by the sword, or death by drowning. But He who never fails nor forsakes had stood by Paul in this dark hour, strengthening and inspiring him with hope so that Paul could say in the light of utter hopelessness, "I believe God."

O Lord, I know that I belong to You. Moreover, I find my greatest delight in serving You. Therefore, Lord, I believe You. The waves of conflict are rolling over me. It seems almost as if there is no hope. And yet this morning You told me that You had sent me to turn men from the power of Satan unto God. As You did for Paul of old, You can do today, even now in my peculiar predicament. Therefore, I believe You. O Lord, help my unbelief. Amen.

"When Paul saw them, he thanked God
and took courage." — Acts 28:15

The journey for Paul had been long and
tedious. Many times the prospect of ever
arriving in Rome had looked bleak. But now
he had landed. Certain brethren had heard of
him and had come out to meet him, and
"when Paul saw them, he thanked God and
took courage."

Those brethren were a definite sign of
encouragement. God sees fit very often to
give His servants signs of blessing for their
encouragement. Those brethren were also the
earnest of the blessing that Paul was going to
see during his time in Rome. Lastly, those
brethren were a fellowship from which he
could expect prayer and cooperation in his
new work.

Give me reason today, Lord, to see the sign,
that I might thank You and take courage.

"Without ceasing I make mention of you." — Romans 1:9

Paul writes these words in the very presence
of God. "For God is my witness," he says (v. 9).
In other words, when he says that he makes
mention of the saints at Rome with unceasing
consistency, he does not exaggerate but tells
the truth. How qualified he was then to write
in another place, "Pray without ceasing"
(1 Thess. 5:17).

Paul knew the importance and power of
persistent prayer. Like his Master, he knew
that "men always ought to pray and not lose
heart" (Luke 18:1).

Note the result and fruit of the unceasing
prayer of Paul: he had heard that their faith
was proclaimed "throughout the whole world"
(Rom. 1:8).

Teach me the discipline of praying without ceasing, Lord.

"In whatever you judge another you condemn yourself;
for you who judge practice the same things."
— Romans 2:1

Here is a law of God. When Paul wrote it or emphasized it, he was addressing the apostate Jew. But as a law, it is applicable to all.

The law in essence is this: I must not practice anything for which I would condemn another. The Lord Himself propounded this same law when he said, "Judge not, that you be not judged. For with what judgment you judge, you will be judged . . . why do you look at the speck in your brother's eye, but do not consider the plank in your own eye?" (Matt. 7:1-3).

Give me the grace, O Lord, to live what I preach.
Help me not to judge, if I would not be judged. Amen.

*"For what if some did not believe? Will their unbelief
make the faithfulness of God without effect? Certainly
not! Indeed, let God be true but every man a liar."*
— Romans 3:3-4

What a verse this is for the man who doubts
the faithfulness of God! God is faithful. It is
His intrinsic quality. God ceases to be God
when He ceases to be faithful. Thus, Paul says
in his second letter to Timothy, "If we are
faithless, He remains faithful; He cannot deny
Himself" (2 Tim. 2:13).

Yes, He is the unchanging One. Jesus Christ,
one with the Father, is the same yesterday
and forever.

Lord, I claim Your faithfulness as the basis of my prayer.
Amen.

"Not while circumcised, but while uncircumcised."
— Romans 4:10

It is when one sees such phrases as this one, that some of the hidden wonders of this marvelous Book are revealed. Paul is propounding the doctrine of the sovereignty of God's grace, and he shows clearly that "by grace you have been saved through faith, and that not of yourselves; it is the gift of God, not of works, lest anyone should boast" (Eph. 2:8-9). To prove his point, he refers back to Abraham, the man who was reckoned for righteousness. He shows that God reckoned the blessing of righteousness to Abraham before he was circumcised. Now circumcision was the work of the law. The operation of circumcision had to be done by man. Thus, if righteousness was imputed to Abraham because of his circumcision, the righteousness would be of works and not of grace. Herein shines the fact that this wondrous Book is inspired. For though Abraham lived centuries before, yet God ruled it that he should be blessed apart from works, thus confirming the teaching of the New Testament.

From beginning to end, how marvelous is Your Word!

"Saved by His life." — Romans 5:10

This is a glorious thought – salvation or reconciliation has not only been made through His death, but also by His life. That is to say, that by dying with Him, I am also raised to live with Him, knowing that Christ being raised from the dead dies no more. As long as He lives, I live; for death has no more dominion over Him.

The apostle really understood this truth when he wrote, "I have been crucified with Christ; it is no longer I who live, but Christ lives in me; and the life which I now live in the flesh I live by faith in the Son of God" (Gal. 2:20). No wonder his great ambition was to know Christ and the power of His Resurrection.

Praise God! The power of the resurrection
is the life over which death has no more dominion.

"Fruit to holiness." — *Romans 6:22*

Before a seed bears fruit, it must first die. Before a believer bears fruit, he must be made free from sin through dying with Christ. "Reckon yourselves to be dead indeed to sin," says the apostle (Rom. 6:11). After death, the seed sprouts into new life. Similarly, if we become united to Christ in His death, we shall be united to Him in His resurrection.

The next essential for a fruit bearing plant is its pruning. The plant, so to speak, must yield itself to the experienced gardener. In the same way, the believer must present himself as alive from the dead, and his members as instruments of righteousness unto God. So that just as that plant now becomes the servant of the gardener, even so the believer becomes the servant of God. Thus says the apostle, "you have your fruit to holiness" (v. 22). This is the fruit of holiness or character: love, joy, peace . . .

O Lord, make me more fruitful for You.

"I would not have known sin except through the law."
— Romans 7:7

The "law" here can mean the whole counsel of God, or rather the whole Word of God. For the Word of God "is profitable for doctrine, for reproof, for correction, for instruction in righteousness" (2 Tim. 3:16). Thus, it is only as I read and study the Word, that I shall have the knowledge of sin. As the Word of God teaches, reproves, and corrects, sin in its many forms is revealed. In this, the law is "holy and just and good" (Rom. 7:12).

As each sin is thus made known, it must immediately be crucified – reckoned dead. Thus, one's life is progressively and practically sanctified to bring forth more fruit.

O Lord, reveal sin to me in its real light,
then show me my Savior. Amen.

"For if you live according to the flesh you will die."
— Romans 8:13

Farther up in the chapter, Paul writes, "To be
carnally minded is death" (v. 6). The mind here
is that inward principle of sin which is at
enmity against God (the only source of life)
— the principle which cannot be subject to the
law of God or please Him. The fruit (or wages)
of this law or principle is death. "If you live
according to the flesh you will die" (v. 13).
How solemn a truth is this! Nor does it apply
to unbelievers here. On the contrary, its
primary application is to the believer, if he has
the Spirit of Christ.

The death is, of course, the physical death.
The same death that Paul speaks about in
1 Corinthians 11:30, where he says, "For this
reason many are [living after the flesh] weak
and sick among you, and many sleep." Also,
the apostle John in 1 John 5:16 speaks of "sin
leading to death."

O wretched man that I am who shall deliver me
from the body of this death? I thank God
through Jesus Christ my Lord.

*"For the Scripture says to Pharaoh, 'For this very purpose
I have raised you up, that I may show My power in you,
and that My name may be declared in all the earth.'"*
— Romans 9:17

"God moves in a mysterious way His wonders
to perform."[11]

God's purposes must be fulfilled, and He
sometimes uses the very vessels of wrath to
accomplish His great plans.

The apostle Paul illustrates this fact in
referring to Pharaoh. Pharaoh was a vessel of
wrath – one who did not fear God. But even
so, God used him to accomplish His designs.
For through Pharaoh, God demonstrates His
power, thus making known His Name
throughout all the earth. If God can use a
vessel such as Pharaoh, how much more can
He use a vessel sanctified and ready for the
Master's use!

Make me a sanctified and ready vessel, Lord!

"Whoever believes on Him will not be put to shame."
— Romans 10:11

The shame the apostle writes about here is the shame that the Lord Jesus spoke about when He said, "For whoever is ashamed of Me and My words in this adulterous and sinful generation, of him the Son of Man also will be ashamed when He comes in the glory of His Father with the holy angels" (Mark 8:38).

The man who is going to be ashamed is the man who lives a Christ-less life. This applies, in measure, to believers as well, for it is possible to be saved and then to fall back or backslide. The cause of this is unbelief. The above verse declares that it is the man who believes who shall not be ashamed. If there is an evil heart of unbelief, however, there will be shame even for the Christian. "Abide in Him, that . . . we may . . . not be ashamed before Him at His coming" (1 John 2:28).

"Without faith, it is impossible to please Him."
— Hebrews 11:6

EVENING READING: ROMANS 11

"For of Him and through Him and to Him
are all things." — Romans 11:36

"*Of Him.*" He is the creator of all things. "All
things were made through Him, and without
Him nothing was made that was made"
(John 1:3).

"*Through Him.*" He is mediator of all things.
"He who did not spare His own Son . . . how
shall He not with Him also freely give us all
things?" (Rom. 8:32). There is only one
mediator between God and man, the man
Christ Jesus.

"*To Him.*" He is the object for which all things
have been created and mediated. "All things
were created through Him and for Him"
(Col. 1:16). It is for His glory alone that all
things exist.

Lord, I owe my very existence to You, my sustenance
to You, and therefore, I will live for You.

"You present your bodies a living sacrifice, holy, acceptable to God, which is your reasonable service" — Romans 12:1

When the Lord Jesus spoke to the woman of Samaria, He said, "Those who worship Him must worship in spirit and truth" (John 4:24); in other words, spiritually and according to truth. To worship spiritually is to worship under full control of the Holy Spirit. To worship according to truth is to worship according to the knowledge of the Truth. As to the Truth, note that there must be the unreserved presentation of the body:

A *Living Sacrifice*. Spiritually living, quickened from spiritual death.

A *Holy Body*. Separate from all defilement. Cleansed and made acceptable for worship. Thus, the apostle says, "Let a man examine himself" (1 Cor. 11:28).

An *Acceptable Body*. Conformed to God's will.

Were the whole realm of nature mine,
That were a present far too small;
Love so amazing, so divine,
Demands my soul, my life, my all.[12]

Evening Reading: Romans 13

"Make no provision for the flesh, to fulfill its lusts."
— *Romans 13:14*

The flesh is one of the three greatest enemies of the Christian. There is no moment when this enemy is not present, ready to assert itself. And in view of this fact, the apostle says, "Make no provision for the flesh, to fulfill its lusts." Give the flesh no chance whatsoever to fulfill its lusts. The only way to do this is explained in the preceding command: "Put on the Lord Jesus Christ" (v. 14).

This is Ephesians 6:11 – The Armor of God. This armor, it will be observed, is complete. It guards against the World, the flesh, and the Devil. O, to avail myself then of this armor! Paul did when he cried out, "O wretched man that I am! Who will deliver me from this body of death? I thank God – through Jesus Christ our Lord!" (Rom. 7:24-25).

Let me quell my flesh then,
by daily putting on the armor of God.

Morning Reading: Romans 14

"Let each be fully convinced in his own mind."
— Romans 14:5

There are some, says the apostle, which esteem one day above another. Similarly, there are believers who eat certain meats which others would not touch. "Let each be fully convinced in his own mind." This assurance the Holy Spirit will confirm, if the following things serve as the guiding principles:

- Christ must be Lord (v. 8).
- All must be done in the light of the Judgment Seat (v. 10).
- What is done must not cause a brother to stumble (vv. 13, 21).
- It must not overthrow the Work of God (v. 20).
- It must be done in faith; otherwise, it is sin (v. 23).
- My brother must not be judged, as long as what he does is not a stumbling block (v. 13).
- In all, I must follow the things that make for peace and edification (v. 19).

Lord, may I weigh all things against these principles and the assurance of the Holy Spirit.

"For if the Gentiles have been partakers of their spiritual things, their duty is also to minister to them in material things." — Romans 15:27

Paul speaks here of the responsibility of those who have been made partakers of spiritual things. "Their duty," he says, "is also to minister in material things."

The servant of the Lord must be the minister of the spiritual things. He must be faithful in his ministry. But those to whom he ministers must be just as faithful in their ministry of material things. "For the Scripture says, 'You shall not muzzle an ox while it treads out the grain,' and, 'The laborer is worthy of his wages'" (1 Tim. 5:18).

O, that the Church might know its responsibility, Lord.

Morning Reading: Romans 16

*"For those who are such do not serve our Lord Jesus
Christ, but their own belly, and by smooth words and
flattering speech deceive the hearts of the simple."*
— Romans 16:18

O, to be faithful to my Lord and Savior Jesus
Christ! *O, to be so acquainted with the Word of
God that I shall never be deceived by smooth words
and flattering speech. Lord, hear my prayer to You.*

"Such . . . serve . . . their own belly." This applies to
anyone who takes the name of Christian for
ulterior motives, base interests, or sensual
indulgence.

"Smooth words and flattering speech." Is it
any wonder that the apostle declares,
"My speech and my preaching were not with
persuasive words of human wisdom, but in
demonstration of the Spirit and of power, that
your faith should not be in the wisdom of
men but in the power of God" (1 Cor. 2:4-5).

"The hearts of the simple." The unsuspecting —
those who do not test the spirits to see
whether they are of God (1 John 4:1).

Lord, help me to be always alert to the wiles of the Devil.

"For the message of the cross is foolishness to those who are perishing." — 1 Corinthians 1:18

Lord, give me a real passion for perishing sinners. The Word of the cross may be foolishness to many, but there are plenty who long to know Christ has died for their sins according to the Scriptures, that He has been buried, and that He has been raised, according to the Scriptures.

The tragedy is that they are perishing now. *Give a vision, Lord, of a perishing world. Give a vision of Yourself.* For Your Word has taught me that *"where there is no vision, the people perish"* (Prov. 29:18, KJV).

Hear my prayer for Christ's sake. Amen.

"We have the mind of Christ." – 1 Corinthians 2:16

What an assertion for Paul to make! And yet it was true. For further up in the chapter he says, "We have received, not the spirit of the world, but the Spirit who is from God" (v. 12) – the same Holy Spirit which reveals all things. "The Spirit searches all things, yes, the deep things of God" (v. 10).

In another place, Paul says, "Let this mind be in you which was also in Christ Jesus" (Phil. 2:5). The context then reveals that it is the mind of humility, which is the beauty of holiness, without which no man can see God. Peter says (looking back on the occasion which is recorded in John 13), "Gird up your minds with the towel of humility." The words of Christ Himself were, "Learn from Me, for I am gentle and lowly in heart" (Matt. 11:29) – this is the mind of Christ.

O, to be filled and controlled by the Searching
Spirit. Only thus can I hope to know
the mind of God and Christ.

"All things are yours." — *1 Corinthians 3:21*

"He who did not spare His own Son, but delivered Him up for us all, how shall He not with Him also freely give us all things?" (Rom. 8:32). How wonderful to think and know that through Christ, I personally am entitled to all things, whether they be human, material, living, dead, present things or things to come. No man of the world can make this assertion. He may assume that all things are his and, because of God's lovingkindness, he may in a measure enjoy them; but actually all things belong only to Christians.

But what is mine is Christ's and Christ's God's. I am not my own, I am Christ's, for He has bought me.

"Take myself, and I will be ever only all for Thee."[13]

"But with me it is a very small thing that I should be judged by you or by a human court. . . . He who judges me is the Lord." — 1 Corinthians 4:3

The hallmark of true stewardship is faithfulness. The words of my blessed Lord in that day will be, "Well done, good and faithful [not successful] servant" (Matt. 25:21). True faithfulness is heart attitude before God. "Without faith it is impossible to please Him" (Heb. 11:6). "Whatever is not from faith is sin" (Rom. 14:23). Faithfulness, then, can be judged by my own heart attitude to God — or fellowship with Him. As long as that fellowship is maintained, I please Him, and this is faithfulness. When that fellowship is broken through the intrusion of sin or straying out of the path of light, the fellowship is broken and I can know it. Therefore, the apostle could say, "It is a very small thing that I should be judged by you or by a human court. In fact, I do not even judge myself. For I know nothing against myself, yet I am not justified by this; but He who judges me is the Lord" (1 Cor. 3-4).

When that time arrives, may You judge me to have been good and faithful. Amen.

*"When you are gathered together, along with my spirit,
with the power of our Lord Jesus Christ, deliver such
a one to Satan."* — 1 Corinthians 5:4-5

The absolute essentials for such an action as
delivering one to Satan for the destruction of
the flesh, or the precise converse – the
deliverance of a man from the bondage of
Satan – are these:

Believers must own His Presence. They must be
gathered in the name of the Lord Jesus. "For
where two or three are gathered together in
My name, I am there in the midst of them"
(Matt. 18:20). *Believers must own His Presidency,*
i.e., agreed together on His joy, presidence
(lordship), in the action that is to be taken.
Believers must own His Power. His power on the
basis of all He has accomplished and said; His
blood and Word. For after finishing the work
God gave him to do, the risen Christ said, "All
power is given unto me in heaven and in
earth" (Matt. 28:18, KJV).

May I live and serve under Your authority
and in the light of Your presence.

"God both raised up the Lord and will also raise us up by His power." — 1 Corinthians 6:14-15

"All things," says the apostle, "are lawful for me, but all things are not helpful. All things are lawful for me, but I will not be brought under the power of any" (v. 12). The power he speaks about here is not in himself, but the power of God which raised the Lord.

The Lord Jesus voluntarily took upon Himself the load of sin. It bore Him down to death, even the death of the Cross (the lower depths). But from such depths, Christ was raised by the power of God. Is it difficult then to see that with that same power God can and will raise me up from the burdens, depths, and bondage that sin would bring? How much more, too, the very things that are lawful, which can and do sometimes bind with their power. God can bring such things to naught.

What power and love! Praise His Name!

*"Brethren, let each one remain with God in that state
in which he was called." — 1 Corinthians 7:24*

Here is a message to my own heart: find
contentment in the things I have and the
ministry to which He has called me.

This requires patience. For very often, my
calling requires waiting periods. O, to know
the truth of the words, "They also serve who
only stand and wait."[14]

This calling also requires consistency. It is so
easy to be spasmodic in Christian service,
especially when circumstances lend
themselves to extra efforts. But to be
consistent and patient necessitates God.
Hence, the apostle says, "Remain with God"
(v. 24). "If God is for us, who can be against
us?" (Rom. 8:31).

No wonder Moses said, "If Your Presence does
not go with us, do not bring us up from here"
(Ex. 33:15).

*Teach me, Lord, to be content with such things as I have,
and in the vocation wherewith I am called.*

"Knowledge puffs up, but love edifies."
— *1 Corinthians 8:1*

The power of this spiritual truth is evidenced by its practical outworking. The apostle tells us that their "love suffers long and is kind; . . . is not puffed up; . . . thinks no evil" (1 Cor. 13:4-5).

O, then to excel in this essential. Its secret lies in the work of the Holy Spirit, for He sheds abroad the love of God in the heart of the believer. Moreover, the fruit of the Spirit is love. O, to be filled with the Holy Spirit, moment by moment, day by day.

Then, and only then, shall my ministry be edifying, building up believers in grace and in the knowledge of the Lord Jesus Christ.

The love of Christ compels us to live, teach, and preach Christ in love.

Holy Spirit, fill me with the love of Jesus Christ.

"I buffet [bruise] my body, and bring it into bondage:
lest by any means, after that I have preached to others,
I myself should be rejected." – 1 Corinthians 9:27 ASV

The apostle presents a dreadful possibility in
this verse by way of warning. The possibility is
to preach to others (i.e., run in the race) then
be rejected for a reward. The great danger is
implied in the words, "I bruise my body." In
other words, the supremacy of the flesh can
disqualify a man in the race of service. The
flesh – that I, or self – the great enemy of
every believer.

"I bruise my body," he says. To bruise is to sap
the life out of anything. My blessed Lord was
bruised for me (Isa. 53:5) on the cross of
Calvary. And that is just where this body must
hang by faith, if it is to be crucified.

May my testimony be that I have been
crucified with Christ.

"Nor let us commit sexual immorality . . . nor let us tempt Christ . . . nor complain." – 1 Corinthians 10:8-10

There are three sins pointed out in these verses that called down the judgment of the Lord upon those old pilgrims.

The Sin of Indulgence. They committed fornication. Their vile passions changed the natural use of their bodies into that which is against nature. The wages of this sin was death. *The Sin of Infestation.* They tempted, tested, or tried the Lord. This was a deliberate transgression of the commandment, "You shall not tempt the Lord your God" (Deut. 6:16). The wages of this sin was also death. *The Sin of Ingratitude.* Of all sins, this is the worst. It is the sin which the Devil introduced to Eve, when he said, "Has God indeed said" (Gen. 3:1) – casting a doubt on the goodness of God. Thus the apostle says, "Do you despise the riches of His goodness . . . you are treasuring up for yourself wrath in the day of wrath and revelation of the righteous judgment of God" (Rom. 2:4). The people of Israel murmured against God's goodness and they perished!

Lord, keep sin far from me – all sin, every sin.

"Do this in remembrance of Me." — 1 Corinthians 11:24

This remembrance feast is the portion and privilege of every company of God's people, from the two's and three's to the large churches of God. It is a unique remembrance feast of a united and individual:

- *Appropriation of the Lord*
  (Body & Blood)
- *Annunciation of the Lord*
  (In His Death)
- *Anticipation of the Lord*
  (In His Coming)

Appropriation of the Body and Blood of the Lord Jesus Christ. "As often as you eat this bread and drink this cup" (1 Cor. 11:26).

Annunciation of the Death of the Lord Jesus Christ. "You proclaim the Lord's death" (v. 26).

Anticipation of the Coming Again of the Lord Jesus. "Till He comes" (v. 26).

Enable me, O Lord, Sunday by Sunday to enter more into the meaning of this wonderful remembrance feast.

"Now concerning spiritual gifts . . ." – 1 Corinthians 12:1

"There are diversities of gifts" (v. 4). The apostle Paul enumerates seven of these gifts in verses 28 and 29. But there are many gifts. The believer's responsibility, however, is to desire earnestly the greater gifts. The Holy Spirit is the direct source.

"There are differences of ministries" (v. 5). But just as the Holy Spirit is the direct source of these gifts, even so the Lord's service is the only sphere in which those gifts can be exercised as ministries.

"There are diversities of activities" (v. 6). In the first thought, the Spirit's work is preeminent. In the second thought, it is the Son. Here, it is the Father. He is the great Worker "who works all in all" (v. 6). He binds together the work of the Spirit, Son, and Himself into one purpose – the edifying of the Church.

Manifest Your purpose in my life, O Lord.

Evening Reading: 1 Corinthians 13

"Love." — 1 Corinthians 13:4

The apostle says, "Now abide faith, hope, love, these three; but the greatest of these is love" (v. 13). A little further up he gives the negative and positive definitions of love:

Negative (vv. 4-8): Love does not envy; Love does not parade itself; Love is not puffed up; Love does not behave rudely; Love does not seek its own; Love is not provoked; Love thinks no evil; Love does not rejoice in iniquity; and Love never fails.

Positive (vv. 4-7): Love suffers long; Love is kind; Love rejoices in the truth; Love bears all things; Love believes all things; Love hopes all things; and, Love endures all things.

O Lord, shed abroad the love of God in my heart, for Christ's sake. Amen.

"Let all things be done decently and in order."
— *1 Corinthians 14:40*

The literal translation of this verse is "Let all things be done becomingly and according to arrangement." What an exhortation to all who seek to run or organize the concerns of God! First, all things must be done as "becoming" the Lord, worthy of the Lord, and His glory. How careful one ought to be then to see that nothing in any way casts dishonor on what is done for Him. Second, "according to arrangement" does away with all the well-worn ideas about no pre-arranged plans necessary. The teaching here is clear that order and arrangement must characterize all that is done for God.

In my life and ministry, Lord, let all things be done
"decently and in order."

"I labored . . . yet not I, but the grace of God
which was with me." – 1 Corinthians 15:10

How forcibly I am reminded of that other
Scripture which reads like this one: "It is no
longer I who live, but Christ lives in me"
(Gal. 2:20).

In that Galatian Scripture, it is "Christ
Supreme" in life. Here, it is "Christ Supreme"
in service. Paul could say, "By the grace of
God, I am what I am" (1 Cor. 15:10). Grace had
changed him, grace had made him, and now
grace was using him.

"I labored . . . yet not I, but the grace" (v. 10).
"For you know the grace of our Lord Jesus
Christ, that though He was rich, yet for your
sakes He became poor, that you through His
poverty might become rich" (2 Cor. 8:9). This
is grace – self-depreciation, self-abnegation,
self-sacrifice – for the blessing of others.

"Grace, grace, God's grace . . ."[15] *May such grace be at work*
in and through my life and service.

"Watch, stand fast in the faith, be brave, be strong."
— *1 Corinthians 16:13*

These four commands have a definite order and lead up to the last one – "Be strong." The fulfilling of these four commands was, no doubt, the secret of Paul's strength.

Be Watchful. He merely emphasizes the words of the Lord Jesus, when He said, "Watch and pray – lest you enter into temptation" (Matt. 26:41). Spiritual vigilance enables the Christian to prepare for victorious battles.

Be Stable. Here is a call to consistency, to establishment, to stability – holding the profession of faith without wavering.

Be Manlike. To be a real man, the spirit, soul, and body must be equally nourished.

Be Strong. This is the natural outcome of watchfulness, stability, and manliness. It results in being strong for God, strong against the powers of evil, and strong in the Lord.

Lord, may these commands be characteristic of my walk with You.

EVENING READING: 2 CORINTHIANS 1

"You also helping together in prayer for us, that thanks may be given by many persons on our behalf for the gift granted to us through many." — 2 Corinthians 1:11

This verse shows a little of what real intercessory prayer can do. Paul speaks of their prayer on his behalf. Here were believers who realized their responsibility in prayer. Moreover, such a responsibility and the meeting of it brought remarkable results. Notice, "the gift granted to us through many." As a result of intercessory prayer, the apostle, with his colleagues, experienced the endowment of a real gift. The gift was such that in holiness, sincerity, and grace, God used them mightily in the church at Corinth.

O, to never neglect to intercede for others in my daily prayers!

"If indeed I have forgiven anything, I have forgiven that
one for your sakes in the presence of Christ, lest Satan
should take advantage of us; for we are not ignorant
of his devices." — 2 Corinthians 2:10-11

> Kind and tender and forgiving,
> God in Christ has been to me;
> So should we, to one another,
> Kind and tenderhearted be.

It is very clear from what Paul says, that the
Devil gains great advantages over believers on
the subject of the "Unforgiving Spirit." Paul,
and saints ever since, could say, "We are not
ignorant of his devices" (2 Cor. 2:11). One
only has to look at some meetings, homes, or
certain individuals, and one can see what the
devices of Satan have wrought through the
medium of the unforgiving spirit.

So, Paul teaches the right spirit that should
be adopted in relation to the question of
forgiving: "I have forgiven . . . in the presence
of Christ."

Lord, give me this forgiving spirit. Amen.

EVENING READING: 2 CORINTHIANS 3

*"Therefore, since we have such hope, we use
great boldness of speech." — 2 Corinthians 3:12*

The hope that the apostle speaks of here is the
lasting glory of the Lord Jesus Christ, who
brought grace and truth in place of the Law
of Moses.

Knowing then that such a glory awaits the
believer, the apostle speaks of this hope as that
which emboldens speech.

The transforming power of that glory can be
experienced even now in a measure (v. 18).
But it is only as the believer reflects the glory
by beholding the Lord in the Word through
the Holy Spirit.

This grand fact, added to the hope of the yet
greater glory, should and must call forth from
my soul, bold and definite testimony.

*The joy of Your grace and truth cannot be contained —
I am compelled to speak of it boldly!*

"Therefore, since we have this ministry, as we have received mercy, we do not lose heart." — 2 Corinthians 4:1

O Lord, this is a real message for my heart! And as I prepare for service, I would do so, insomuch as I have obtained mercy, for I am conscious that I shall otherwise faint ("lose heart").

"Therefore we do not lose heart. Even though our outward man is perishing, yet the inward man is being renewed day by day" (v. 16). This verse is also very encouraging. The mercy is that which brings me into the position where my inward man is renewed and strengthened to compensate the fainting and failing outward man.

I would receive mercy then, from Your loving hand, O Lord. Amen.

"Therefore we make it our aim, whether present or
absent, to be well pleasing to Him." – 2 Corinthians 5:9

This was the apostle's ambition – "to be well
pleasing" to the Lord. And what an ambition!
As to whether he succeeded or not is to be
decided by his Lord in that day. He could say,
however, "I have fought the good fight, I have
finished the race, I have kept the faith. Finally,
there is laid up for me the crown of
righteousness" (2 Tim. 4:7-8). But though he
could say this at the end of his life, he could
only say it because he determined to forget
and press on, never counting to have
apprehended.

This was also my blessed Lord's ambition. He
could say, "I do always those things that please
Him [God]" (John 8:29). God could therefore
say of Him, "This is My beloved Son, in whom
I am well pleased" (Matt. 17:5).

To be well pleasing to You is my desire, Lord.

Morning Reading: 2 Corinthians 6

"You also be open." — 2 Corinthians 6:13

It is not without significance that such words as these should precede a dissertation on separation.

The apostle evidently looked upon those who frequented the idol houses or temples as narrow, limited, tied by such worship as idol worship! And he pleads with them here to "be open." The apostle testifies that his heart was open (v. 11).

The meaning of "You also be open" is stipulated in the following verses:
"Do not be unequally yoked together with unbelievers" (v. 14). This does not mean to not live among or preach to them. On the contrary, it means, "have no fellowship with the unfruitful works of darkness" (Eph. 5:11).

"Come out from among them" (v. 17).
"Do not touch what is unclean" (v. 17).
"Cleanse ourselves from all filthiness" (2 Cor. 7:1).

Lord, help me to guard my life, and anoint my words and works that unbelievers might respond with open hearts.

*"In all things you proved yourselves to be clear
in this matter." – 2 Corinthians 7:11*

The apostle makes no apology for the strong
language that he uses in writing to these
Corinthians. In fact, he does not regret that
his letter has brought sorrow, "For godly
sorrow produces repentance leading to
salvation" (v. 10). This "salvation" was:

- *Diligence.* Earnest care. Concern
  for spiritual things.
- *Clearing of self* – Cleansing.
- *Indignation* – Against sin.
- *Fear* – Godly fear.
- *Vehement desire* – Longing for a
  deeper experience of Christ.
- *Zeal for His glory.*
- *Vindication.* Avenging the Lord's just
  claims.

This seven-fold "salvation" was wrought in
them through the message of Paul by the
Holy Spirit, so that in everything they were
approved and pure.

*When Your Spirit reproves and corrects me, Lord,
teach me to respond in a godly manner, that I may
repent and be clear in all matters.*

"He who gathered much had nothing left over, and he who gathered little had no lack." — 2 Corinthians 8:15

The apostle illustrates his teaching on giving by quoting this Old Testament Scripture. The point he seeks to emphasize is that of equality among the people of God. How little is known of this in the Church today!

In the early chapters of Acts, we read of the disciples having "all things in common" (Acts 2:44). They that had possessions handed them to the apostles, and the apostles to them who served tables that they should distribute to all who were in need.

In other words, God never intends His children to hoard. Thus, the force of the above verse can be readily seen. He that gathered much had *nothing*. It turned into corruption! He that gathered little had *no lack*. Paul could say from experience, "I have learned in whatever state I am, to be content" (Phil. 4:11).

Lord, all that I have comes from You and is Yours even now. Direct me in how You would have me to use it.

"God loves a cheerful giver." — 2 Corinthians 9:7

Giving must not be haphazard. It must be as a man purposes in his own heart before the Lord. It must not be with a grudging heart, but with unstinted love and joy. This is best illustrated in the story of the widow and the two mites. She gave all, not grudgingly, but with cheer and love. Giving must not be the outcome of obvious necessity. In fact, if necessity arises, it is the evidence of grudged giving. The necessity would never arise if believers gave as is laid down in this chapter.

God loves a cheerful giver, and giving is a special love of God, experienced only by those who give purposefully, cheerfully, and regularly.

Make me, Lord, a cheerful giver.

"Bringing every thought into captivity to the obedience of Christ." — 2 Corinthians 10:5

Solomon says, "As [a man] thinks in his heart, so is he" (Prov. 23:7). All issues of life commence with the thought life. How important then to bring every thought into captivity to the obedience of Christ.

The thoughts and imaginations to be brought into captivity are those which exalt themselves *against* the knowledge of God. God, in the person of the Lord Jesus, must be supreme in the life of the believer. And if He is supreme in one's life, He must be Master of one's thoughts as well. For as already observed, thoughts determine the issues of life.

The great example of bringing every thought into captivity to the obedience is given in Philippians 2. Here Christ humbled Himself and became obedient unto death (Phil. 2:8). He did this to bring into captivity the exalted thoughts of sin to the obedience of God. Is it any wonder Paul says, "Let this mind [of Christ] be in you" (Phil. 2:5)?

Teach me, O Lord, to bring all thoughts captive to You.

"Deep concern for all the churches."
— 2 Corinthians 11:28

Herein is an amazing truth! The apostle, in the preceding verses, has numbered some of the sufferings and afflictions that he has endured for the sake of the Lord Jesus. But last of all he adds, "Besides the other things, what comes upon me daily: my deep concern for all the churches" (v. 28).

Paul lived so close to the Lord that he was sensitive to the minutest suffering of any member of the body of Christ. Notice he says "deep concern for all the churches." That included every member. In this verse, Paul proved in practice what he propounds in theory in 1 Corinthians 12 – "if one member suffers, all the members suffer with it" (1 Cor. 12:26).

Does not this explain the mystery of some of the sorrowful times I go through? Do I pray for the suffering ones?

Lord, create in me a spirit so sensitive to suffering that I too develop a deep concern.

"Most gladly I will rather boast in my infirmities, that the power of Christ may rest [cover, or spread a tabernacle over me] upon me." — 2 Corinthians 12:9

While the truth contained in this verse is practical, it is not automatic. That is to say, that while the believer is made strong in weakness, he does not merit the power of Christ on the grounds of his becoming weak. This power cannot be bought or merited.

When Paul speaks of boasting here, he is not unmindful of the fact that he that glories must glory in the Lord (see 2 Cor. 10:17).

So when Christ is glorified in the emptied dependent life of the believer, it is then that the power of Christ rests upon him.

Christ was glorified in His death, that the power of God might be manifest.

Thank you, Lord, that Your power is manifested in the midst of my weakness. Amen.

"I write these things being absent, lest being present
I should use sharpness, according to the authority
which the Lord has given me for edification and
not for destruction." — 2 Corinthians 13:10

Paul speaks here of *sharpness* and *authority*
which the Lord had given him for edification
and not destruction.

It is very significant that he definitely says,
"For edification and not for destruction"
(v. 10). Paul may have been a severe man of
God – one who could exert authority with
sharpness – but what he said was always
constructive and not destructive. Moreover,
there is not a shadow of a doubt that all was
done in love. For Paul could never write words
like 1 Corinthians 13 and then not practice it.
Moreover, "Knowledge puffs up, but love
edifies" or builds up (1 Cor. 8:1).

Lord, make me a constructive teacher.

"I did not immediately confer with flesh and blood."
— Galatians 1:16

Paul was not a man who was easily persuaded by man. In fact, he would never be influenced at the expense of right. Notice verse 10: "If I still pleased men, I would not be a bondservant of Christ."

When God revealed Christ in him and his eyes were opened, he did not immediately confer with flesh and blood, but went exactly where God led him. Surely, here lay the great power of the apostle. He was not dependent on the support of others, but was entirely dependent on God from the very beginning of his ministry. He was not one to pander to the flesh or popularity of others. He took all his orders from God.

Thank You for reminding me that it is You I serve,
and not those who seek to influence me
with position or power.

EVENING READING: GALATIANS 2

"I went up by revelation." — Galatians 2:2

Here is a definite instance of guidance by
revelation. Revelation is moreover the work of
the Holy Spirit. He is the Spirit of Revelation,
and it is only when one is entirely controlled
by Him that one can have a revelation.

"I went up." Paul was obedient to the
revelation, just as he was to the heavenly
vision on the Damascus Road. That which was
so practical in the life of the apostle ought to
be just as practical today. O, that I might know
definite guidance, not only in matters of great
moments, but in the ordinary things as well.

Reveal Your will to me, Lord, day by day.

"The hearing of faith." — Galatians 3:2

Paul says in Romans, "Faith comes by hearing, and hearing by the word of God" (Rom. 10:17). This verse in effect teaches that the Holy Spirit is received by the "hearing of faith" (Gal. 3:2). The Lord Jesus said to Nicodemus, "Unless one is born of water and the Spirit, he cannot enter the kingdom of God" (John 3:5).

I conclude that the spiritual *process* is: The Word enters the heart, faith is begotten, faith receives the Spirit, and a man is born again. Or, the seed of the Word falls into the womb of the heart, there faith lays hold of it and through faith, the Spirit imparts the new life.

Teach me these great truths, dear Lord, that I may be
a faithful minister of the New Covenant.

"Cast out the bondwoman and her son."
— Galatians 4:30

Paul brings the story of Hagar into this portion of his argument as an allegory. He proves that even from that picture, the flesh must be cast out or done away with if true liberty is to be experienced. Paul says, "He who was born according to the flesh then persecuted him who was born according to the Spirit" (v. 29).

Thus, he amplifies this same truth in Romans when he says, "reckon yourselves to be dead indeed to sin, but alive to God in Christ Jesus our Lord" (Rom. 6:11). If that has been done, "then . . . we are not children of the bondwoman but of the free" (Gal. 4:31).

Blessed Lord, I do pray that I may know experientially this liberty in the Lord.

Morning Reading: Galatians 5

*"Walk in the Spirit, and you shall not fulfill
the lust of the flesh." — Galatians 5:16*

"Walking" presupposes:

Life. So the apostle says, "If we live in the
Spirit, let us also walk in the Spirit" (Gal. 5:15).
There must be the initial life.

Exercise and Effort. This exercise and effort
must not be the *energy of the flesh*; it must
be the *appropriating of faith*, the faith which
appropriates the filling of the Spirit in
obedience to the command, "Be filled with
the Spirit" (Eph. 5:18).

Progress. The man who walks makes progress.
This walking is in contrast to standing still.
Moreover, progress is the admission of failure.
He who sees no failure in his life makes no
progress. Progress in the spiritual sense is
progress in the personal experience of the
Holy Spirit. And when He overcomes failure
in one's life, then there is no more fulfilling of
the lusts of the flesh.

May I walk, O Lord, daily by Your side.

*"If a man is overtaken in any trespass, you who are
spiritual restore such a one." — Galatians 6:1*

Here is a truth that needs emphasizing in the
Church today. Indeed, it needs to be stressed
in one's personal life, too. How easy it is to
condemn a brother who has been overtaken
in some trespass. But we are told, "Judge not,
that you be not judged" (Matt. 7:1), and
"restore such a one in a spirit of gentleness"
(Gal. 6:1).

The failure to do this lies in the fact that there
are few real spiritual Christians today. "You
who are spiritual," says the apostle (v. 1). In
other words, "You that are Spirit-filled." And
no one can be Spirit-filled without exhibiting
the fruits of the Spirit.

One of these fruits is gentleness. For restoring
a brother, this spirit of gentleness must be
exhibited. Jesus was the gentlest man in all
the earth (see also Matt. 11:26).

*Lord, may I always remember Your gentleness
and restoration on my behalf when I encounter
someone overcome by sin.*

"The spirit of wisdom and revelation." — Ephesians 1:17

The apostle says that his great ambition was to know Christ and the power of His resurrection. Peter closes his epistle with the words, "Grow in the grace and knowledge of our Lord and Savior Jesus Christ" (2 Pet. 3:18).

In Ephesians 1:17, Paul teaches that the only way to increase in "the knowledge of Him [Christ]" is through the Spirit of wisdom and revelation.

Wisdom. "The fear of the Lord is the beginning of wisdom" (Psalms 111:10). In other words, reverencing or having regard for the Lord is the beginning of wisdom. The Spirit of wisdom deepens this reverence into a real experience of God.

Revelation. This is the communication to the believer of God's divine will by the operation of the Holy Spirit.

O, that You would fill me with Your Spirit of wisdom and revelation, Lord!

*"For we are His workmanship, created in Christ Jesus
for good works, which God prepared beforehand that we
should walk in them." — Ephesians 2:10*

There are three very important truths revealed
in this verse, and each is related to the
believer.

The believer's life is a purposeful life. Some seem
to think that this is not the case. They live life
aimlessly. But no, there is a purpose in every
Christian's life: it is for good works. "His own
special people, zealous for good works"
(Titus 2:14).

The believer's life is a planned life. Just as our
blessed Lord's life, so the Christian's is a
planned life. And it is for the believer to seek
to know the plan that he might follow it.

The believer's life is a possible life. The words "that
we should walk in them" would not be there if
this life were impossible. "With God all things
are possible" (Matt. 19:26).

*The closer I walk with You, Lord, the more I understand
the work You have purposed for me.*

"For this reason I bow my knees." — Ephesians 3:14

This may be taken spiritually or literally. Just as it appears on the surface, I should take it literally, that Paul, who was a great man of prayer, spent much time on his knees.

On my knees is the place of humble submission. Paul knew what it was to humble himself under the mighty hand of God. Submission or utter weakness is the first essential in prayer. Where this is absent, there is no prayer. For prayer is the admission of weakness. Thus, Paul could say from experience, "When I am weak, then I am strong" (2 Cor. 12:10).

On my knees is the place of humble supplication. Here the apostle learned the art of intercessory prayer. Prayer for the whole family of God, in heaven and on earth!

On my knees is a place of humble surrender. It was on His knees that Christ surrendered His life for sacrifice (Luke 22:41).

Lord, the most powerful place
I can be of service to You is on my knees.

"Let no corrupt word proceed out of your mouth, but what is good for necessary edification." — Ephesians 4:29

What a standard! And yet, one that is obviously possible or else it would not be an injunction to believers.

Just what "corrupt" speech means is best explained in Ephesians 5:3-4: "But fornication and all uncleanness or covetousness, let it not even be named among you, as is fitting for saints; neither filthiness, nor foolish talking, nor coarse jesting, which are not fitting." This is the negative side.

As to the positive, speech should be "good for necessary edification" (Eph. 4:29). If this were the one object in a Christian's life, what a power for God he would be! Setting watch upon his lips, guarding the tongue, meeting every need with words that edify.

O, for grace to do this, Lord.

"Be imitators of God." – Ephesians 5:1

But for the grace and enabling power of God, how utterly impossible to live such a verse! "Imitators of God" – God is life, light, and love. Moreover, even these intrinsic qualities are incomprehensible apart from the Lord Jesus Christ. "No one has seen God at any time. The only begotten Son, who is in the bosom of the Father, He has declared Him" (John 1:18). Therefore, I can only imitate God as I see God revealed or declared in Christ.

God as Life. (Spirit) The whole of Christ's life was lived and controlled in the power of the Eternal Spirit. O, to be filled with the Spirit.

God as Light. He says, "Be holy for I am holy" (1 Pet. 1:16). Christ was holy, harmless, undefiled, separate from sinners.

God as Love. He "so loved . . . that He gave" (John 3:16). Christ so loved the Church that He gave. The essence of love is to give. All that I can give is myself.

O Lord, help me to imitate Your life,
Your light, and Your love. Amen.

"Commandment with promise." — Ephesians 6:2

The apostle states that the command given in verse 1, "Children, obey your parents in the Lord, for this is right," is the first one to carry a promise with it. Now elsewhere, the apostle teaches that all promises are Yes and Amen through the Lord Jesus Christ (2 Cor. 1:20), and also that what God promises He also performs (Rom. 4:21). So with that in view, it is very instructive to note that the twofold promise is:

- "That it may be well with you" (Eph. 6:2) – Prosperity of Life.
- "You may live long on the earth" (Eph. 6:2) – Perpetuity of Life.

The first coincides with the first half of the command "Obey your parents." Obedience is the absolute willing and unreserved submission to the will of the parents. The second blessing fits in with the second part of the command, "Honor your father and mother" (v. 2). Hold them in respect, in reverence, in Godly fear.

Following Your commandments, Father,
always leads to a life of promise.

"Not in any way terrified by your adversaries."
— Philippians 1:28

In the first place, Paul introduces himself as
the bondservant of Christ Jesus and prays that
grace and peace would be the enjoyed portion
of every believer at Philippi. Then, he rejoices
with the believers at the remembrance of
them and admonishes them to go on "still
more and more" in love, knowledge, and
discernment (v. 9). Concerning his own state,
he says, "The things which happened to me
have actually turned out for the furtherance of
the gospel" (v. 12). "The things" being
suffering, bonds, imprisonment, and
praetorian guards. But he glories because the
gospel is being preached there in Rome.
From his own experience then, he draws the
illustration and application to force home the
above verse. He says, in effect, "Do not be
frightened by the adversaries, for we are not
only called to believe, but to suffer!" And
while suffering spells perdition to the
enemies, it is a token of salvation to the
believers.

No matter my circumstances,
may I look for opportunities to further the Gospel.

"You shine as lights in the world, holding fast the word of life." — Philippians 2:15-16

The Lord Jesus said when here upon earth, "Let your light so shine before men, that they may see your good works and glorify your Father in heaven" (Matt. 5:16). Here, the apostle speaks of those lights as the Word of Life. To shine, therefore, the Word of Life must be first practiced (lived), then preached.

Practiced – in the daily round and common task, being doers of the Word. The Lord Jesus was Prophet, mighty in deed (first) and Word (second) (see Luke 24:19). Living the Word, and then preaching and teaching it.

Preached – to those who are in darkness and under the shadow of death; to those who are being blinded by the false and blinding teaching of today.

O, make me shine, Lord!

Morning Reading: Philippians 3

*"To the degree that we have already attained,
let us walk by the same rule." — Philippians 3:16*

New revelations from the Word of God carry
with them heavy responsibility. For "to the
degree that we have already attained," says the
apostle, "let us walk by the same rule."

The principle here, in effect, is the same as
that contained in the words, "Sin is not
imputed when there is no law" (Rom. 5:13).
The Lord Jesus said when here upon earth,
"If I had not come and spoken to them, they
would have no sin, but now they [those who
rejected Christ and His teaching] have no
excuse for their sin" (John 15:22).

So for every new revelation of truth, there is
the corresponding responsibility to walk
according to the revealed truth ("the same
rule"). So James says, "Be doers of the word,
and not hearers only, deceiving yourselves. . . .
He who looks into the perfect law of liberty
and continues in it, and is not a forgetful
hearer but a doer of the word, this one will be
blessed in what he does" (James 1:22, 25).

*O, that I may be faithful to always walk
according to the Truth You have revealed to me.*

*"A sweet–smelling aroma, an acceptable sacrifice,
well pleasing to God." – Philippians 4:18*

Paul uses this beautiful word picture to
describe the gift that he had received from the
Church at Philippi. The picture, of course, is
borrowed from the temple offerings. He sees
their gift being accepted by God, as that sweet
smelling incense which arose before the holy
place to God in the temple. Gifts in the sight
of God are:

Pleasant Fragrances. They rise into His presence
as the incense in the temple arose to Him.

Acceptable Sacrifices. Whatever is true sacrifice
is acceptable to God, for true sacrifice is the
real expression of love.

Well-pleasing. Such gifts receive the Divine
approval of God.

*Lord, let all that I do be a sweet, pleasing,
and acceptable gift to You.*

MORNING READING: COLOSSIANS 1

"That in all things He may have the preeminence."
— Colossians 1:18

Whether they are thrones, dominions, principalities, or powers, He is before all things and in Him all things consist. He is the Preeminent One. He *must* occupy the place of preeminence. He *will* occupy the place of preeminence. For God "has highly exalted Him and given Him the name which is above every name, that at the name of Jesus every knee should bow . . . and that every tongue should confess that Jesus Christ is Lord" (Phil. 2:9-11) – the "Preeminent One."

Even so, in the life of the believer, "in all things," He *must* have the preeminence. The word "all" indicates *every* detailed aspect in the life of the believer. Where He is preeminent, there the fullness of God dwells.

Lord, daily I will give You preeminence in my life. Amen.

*"In whom are hidden all the treasures of wisdom
and knowledge." — Colossians 2:3*

Christ is the One in whom are hid all the
treasures of wisdom and knowledge. He is the
eternal "Logos." He is not only the *thought* of
God, but the expression of that thought as
well. Indeed, He is the full expression of the
"depth of the riches" (Rom. 11:33), both of the
wisdom and knowledge of God.

Moreover, through His servant James, God
has declared, "If any of you lacks wisdom, let
him ask of God, who gives to all liberally and
without reproach" (James 1:5).

*O, then to be an inheritor of the treasures of wisdom and
knowledge! O, to know the One in whom they are hid!
He who said, "I am the truth."*

"You serve the Lord Christ." – Colossians 3:24

How this sentence lifts up the honor and privilege of service! "You serve the Lord Christ." What a person to serve – the Lord Christ!

Serving the Lord – owning His *Divine Mastership.* "No one can serve two masters," said the Lord, "for either he will hate the one and love the other, or else he will be loyal to the one and despise the other" (Matt. 6:24). To own true mastership is to acknowledge one master. In this case, it is the Lord.

Serving the Christ – owning His *Divine Majesty.* He is the Anointed One, the Sent One, the Divine One, the Prophet, Priest, and King. As a subject of the King, I owe Him not only my unreserved service and allegiance, but also all that I have.

O Lord, I do thank You for calling me into such a service!
O, to serve You more faithfully. Amen.

"Take heed to the ministry which you have received in the Lord, that you may fulfill it." — Colossians 4:17

Here is an exhortation for my own heart. How failing one can be in the work of the ministry! It is possible to compromise. It is possible to bury the talent altogether! But here is a message which warns, "Take heed . . . you have received . . . fulfill it."

Take Heed. Here the apostle warns to take heed "that no one may take your crown" (Rev. 3:11). It is going to be tragic to find that after having preached to others, one is found to be a castaway.

You have Received. The Holy Spirit is the direct source of the spiritual gifts, and all believers possess a gift.

Fulfill it. The responsibility of the believer is to use it. Exercise the gifts.

Teach me, Lord, to make full use of the gifts You have given me to further Your kingdom. Amen.

*"For our gospel did not come to you in word only,
but also in power, and in the Holy Spirit and in much
assurance [fullness]." — 1 Thessalonians 1:5*

The apostle Paul tells his son (in the faith), Timothy, to "Preach the Word" (2 Tim. 4:2). Moreover, "Faith comes by hearing, and hearing by the word of God" (Rom. 10:17). Again, rebirth is effected by the incorruptible seed of the Word. But here, says Paul, "Our gospel did not come to you in word only." There was that which accompanied the preaching of the Word:

Power. Not only power in delivery, which is essential, but power inasmuch as the Gospel is the power of God or dynamic of God "for everyone who believes" (Rom. 1:16). *The Holy Spirit.* He is the source of power. "Where the Spirit of the Lord is, there is liberty" (2 Cor. 3:17). Where He works – there is fruit. *Conviction.* That is what is really meant by the word "assurance." The preaching carried conviction. Conviction must precede conversion.

*O, that I might "Preach the Word"
with the conviction and power of the Holy Spirit!*

"You are witnesses." — 1 Thessalonians 2:10

Paul's life was such that he could boldly say, "You are witnesses, and God also, how devoutly and justly and blamelessly we behaved ourselves among you who believe" (v. 10). How much like his Lord! The Lord Jesus could say, "Which of you convicts Me of sin?" (John 8:46).

He uses three words to describe the character of his behavior when at Thessalonica:

Holy. This was in relation to God. He says, "Be holy, for I am holy" (1 Peter 1:16).

Righteous. This was in relation to his own life. "He leads me in the paths of righteousness" (Ps. 23:3).

Unblameable. This was in relation to the outside world, other believers, etc. He was blameless.

Lord, let my life be a testimony of holiness, righteousness, and blamelessness.

"Timothy, our brother and minister of God,
and our fellow laborer in the gospel of Christ."
— 1 Thessalonians 3:2

Timothy must have been a godly young man!
Paul seems to praise him whenever he has a
chance to do so. Writing to the Philippians,
Paul says concerning Timothy, "For I have no
one like-minded . . . as a son with his father he
served with me in the Gospel" (Phil. 2:20, 22).
Timothy was obviously then a very spiritual
young man. One in whom the apostle could
trust.

Thus, Timothy earns this commendation.
"Timothy, our brother and minister of God,
and our fellow laborer in the gospel of Christ."
Fellow laborer – what an honored privilege!
What a commendation!

This was the fruit of learning – to be quiet (for
we do not read of anything that Timothy said),
studying the Scriptures, and practicing its
precepts.

"Be still, and know that I am God."
— Psalm 46:10

"That no one should take advantage of and defraud his brother in this matter, because the Lord is the avenger of all such, as we also forewarned you and testified."
— 1 Thessalonians 4:6

The marginal meaning of the word "defraud" means "to oppress" or "overreach."

It would seem, in the light of the context, that this "defrauding" or "oppressing" is in connection with fornication, or overreaching another brother in the matters of love, courtship, or marriage. Such a thing will be severely judged by the Lord. This is clearly pointed out in the same verse.

But God has called the believer to holiness. His will for him is sanctification: "that each of you should know how to possess his own vessel in sanctification and honor, not in passion of lust, like the Gentiles who do not know God" (1 Thess. 4:4-5).

O, that I might always deal with people with integrity and purity of heart.

*"Putting on the breastplate of faith and love, and as a
helmet the hope of salvation."* — 1 Thessalonians 5:8

Faith, love, and hope are the three principles
that govern the Christian Church as a whole,
the Church locally, and the individual
believer's life. In this verse, these principles
are seen working in the realm of spiritual
warfare. The other two realms in which they
work are the walk of the Christian and the
work of the Christian.

The Breastplate. This portion of the armor of
God (Eph. 6:14) protects the seat of those
vitals in the spiritual life: faith and love. Faith
is the *living link* between God and the
believer. Love is the *dynamic* governing power
in his life. The breastplate protects these in
battle.

The Helmet. This protects the head (Eph. 6:17)
which is the seat of the mind and thoughts –
hope. Where there is no hope, there is no
experience of salvation.

*Help me to daily don this armor, Lord,
as well as teach others to do the same.*

"We are bound to thank God always for you."
— 2 Thessalonians 1:3

The three principles of spiritual life (faith, hope, and love) were so powerful that the apostle, in writing to these Thessalonian believers, had to say, "We are bound to thank God always for you."

He spoke of their *exceeding* faith, *abounding* love, and *patient* hope. Hope, as far as the word is concerned, is not named. But the word "patience" is a word which Paul often used in connection with hope, such as in 1 Thessalonians 1:3 ("patience of hope").

Even under stress and persecution, these three essentials were undimmed. If anything, they were further strengthened, for the apostle speaks of their amazing power of endurance.

Enable me, O Lord, to live so that others
will be bound to give thanks.

*"Because they did not receive the love of the truth,
that they might be saved." — 2 Thessalonians 2:10*

It is significant to note that those who are perishing, and will yet perish, are people who will not receive the love of the Truth. God does not expect a perverse mind to comprehend the Truth, but He does expect a cold heart to melt at the revelation of unutterable love.

Love is the universal language.
It can be understood when words are incomprehensible. Such love, then, can be received or rejected. To receive is to be saved; to reject is to perish.

If there is one lesson I am to learn here, it is that in my presentation of Truth, there should be the outshining of God's love. Therefore, all my preaching must be balanced – grace with truth, law with love, and the Scriptures with the power of God.

*When I testify of You, Lord, let the truth of Your words
be voiced with the love of Your heart. Amen.*

"The Lord direct your hearts into the love of God."
— 2 Thessalonians 3:5

All sin may be summed up in the one word "misdirection." When the Devil came to Eve in the garden, he misdirected the power of her will. Ever since, man has been misdirected.

At conversion a man is "directed" by the power and influence of the Holy Spirit into God's way, along God's will. After conversion, the Christian begins little by little to submit his personality to the directing power of God, so that instead of running contrary to the will of God, he is now released in the right direction for the glory of God.

So the apostle writes here: "The Lord direct your hearts into the love of God."

I worship thee, sweet will of God,
And all thy ways adore;
And every day I live, I long
To love thee more and more.[16]

"I thank Christ Jesus our Lord who has enabled me."
— *1 Timothy 1:12*

What a source of encouragement Paul found in this verse! Though before he was a blasphemer, a persecutor, and injurious, now he is a faithful apostle of Christ Jesus according to the commandment of God.

The enabling power and grace of the Lord is one of the most precious gifts of God to the minister of the Gospel. For unless we are enabled by the Lord, preaching, teaching, or personal soul-winning is hopeless.

When the Lord Jesus called His disciples, He said, "Follow Me, and I will make you [enable you to] become fishers of men" (Mark 1:17).

This enabling grace, which abounded exceedingly toward Paul, consists of faith on one hand and love on the other. These two represent life and power.

Anoint me, O Lord, with Your enabling grace
that I may share Your Word with others.

"Pray everywhere, lifting up holy hands,
without wrath and doubting." – 1 Timothy 2:8

The apostle shows that the three conditions to prayer are holy hands, the absence of wrath, and the absence of doubting.

Holy Hands. This must not be taken literally, of course. The meaning behind this phrase is "holy living." "A conscience without offense toward God and men" (Acts 24:16).

The Absence of Wrath. Having a forgiving spirit, loving one another.

The Absence of Doubting. Having no unbelief. Strong in faith. "He who doubts is like a wave of the sea driven and tossed by the wind. For let not that man suppose that he will receive anything from the Lord" (James 1:6-7).

Remind me, O Lord, to come to Your throne with a clean
heart, a forgiving spirit, and a strong faith. Amen.

"A good work." — 1 Timothy 3:1

Paul calls the office of a bishop (or overseer) "a good work." The qualifications for this office are interesting and important to note.

Positive
- Without reproach • The husband of one wife
- Temperate • Sober-minded
- Orderly • Given to hospitality
- Able to teach • Ruling his house well
- Having a good testimony from those without
- Gentle

Negative
- Not given to wine • Not violent
- Not quarrelsome • Not a lover of money
- Not a novice

There are then ten positive qualifications and five negative. Truly, a high standard, yet it is God's standard. The secret of a well-behaved church lies in the moral qualities as well as spiritual qualities of the oversight. God calls this work "a good work."

No matter my role in the church, Lord, let me always demonstrate these godly characteristics.

EVENING READING: 1 TIMOTHY 4

"Do not neglect the gift that is in you." — 1 Timothy 4:14

1 Corinthians 12 makes it very plain that every believer has a gift given by the Holy Spirit. Therefore, this exhortation comes home to every heart, and indeed, my heart. "Do not neglect the gift that is in you."

The Lord Jesus told a very sad parable of the man who buried his talent in the ground. This is possible in my life and possible in any life. "Look to yourselves," says John, "that we do not lose those things we worked for" (2 John 1:8). The apostle Paul warns also, saying, "Hold fast what you have, that no one may take your crown" (Rev. 3:11), "Stir up the gift of God which is in you" (2 Tim. 1:6), and "Do not neglect the gift that is in you" (1 Tim. 4:14).

O, that I may faithfully exercise the gift
You have purposed for me!

"Keep yourself pure." — *1 Timothy 5:22*

The apostle gives this exhortation twice in this same chapter. First, it is in connection with speaking to sisters, and then in identifying oneself with men generally.

The principle behind this injunction is this: "To the pure all things are pure" (Titus 1:15). That is to say, if I am personally pure in my life and outlook, my connections with others, whether saved or unsaved, or with men or women, it will be "with all purity" (1 Tim. 5:2).

Surely, this is what the Lord Jesus meant when He said, "If therefore your eye is good, your whole body will be full of light" (Matt. 6:22). That is the eye of purity.

Of course, this purity involves moral, physical, and spiritual purity.

Lord, help me to live pure before the world
so that Your light will shine forth.

"Godliness with contentment is great gain."
— *1 Timothy 6:6*

Godliness is really "Christ-likeness." Hence,
Paul writes, "great is the mystery of godliness:
God was manifest in the flesh" (1 Tim. 3:16).
And to the attainment of Godliness or Christ-
likeness, the apostle could say, "I count all
things loss . . . that I may gain Christ" (Phil.
3:8). This life is "great gain" (1 Tim. 6:6).

Contentment is "having food and clothing"
(1 Tim. 6:8) – the bare necessities of life. And
these must not be worried over, for Christ
said, "Do not worry about your life, what you
will eat . . . what you will put on" (Matt. 6:25).
He provides both food and clothing.

Thus, both godliness and contentment are to
be found in Him. This is great gain!

*"Godliness is profitable for all things, having promise of
the life that now is and of that which is to come."*
— *1 Timothy 4:8*

*"To which I was appointed a preacher, an apostle,
and a teacher of the Gentiles." – 2 Timothy 1:11*

It is interesting to note the order in which
Paul states his capacity: preacher, apostle, and
teacher.

He calls this "a holy calling . . . according to
[God's] own purpose and grace" (2 Tim. 1:9).

As a Preacher – Paul could say, "Necessity is laid
upon me; yes, woe is me if I do not preach the
gospel! (1 Cor. 9:16). "Christ did not send me
to baptize, but to preach the gospel" (1 Cor.
1:17). *As an Apostle* – "For you [Christians] are
the seal of my apostleship in the Lord. . . . For
though I am free from all men, I have made
myself a servant to all, that I might win the
more" (1 Cor. 9:2, 19). *As a Teacher* – He was
supreme, as evidenced by his epistles. Thus,
Paul directs Timothy and us all, "Hold fast the
pattern of sound words which you have heard
from me, in faith and love which are in Christ
Jesus" (2 Tim. 1:13).

*How unsatisfying my life would be, Lord,
were I not to strive to fulfill Your calling!*

*"A servant of the Lord must not quarrel but be gentle
to all, able to teach, patient."* — 2 Timothy 2:24

Here are three definite qualities which should
not be lacking in the true servant of the Lord.
He must not quarrel, but:

Be gentle. This is a fruit of the Spirit, as indeed
are the other two. Gentleness marked the life
of the Lord Jesus. "When He was reviled, did
not revile in return . . . but committed
Himself to Him who judges righteously"
(1 Pet. 2:23).

Be able to teach. Ability implies adaptability;
and the thought here is that the servant of the
Lord is one who adapts himself to all
opportunities.

Be patient. This is love on trial. "Tribulation
produces perseverance" (Rom. 5:3).

O, to be a true servant of the Lord!

"Out of them all the Lord delivered me."
— 2 Timothy 3:11

Paul testifies here to the delivering power of
the Lord. He had endured severe persecutions
and afflictions but, in them all, faith in the
Lord had delivered him.

Paul was one who could glory in infirmities,
in weaknesses, because in them he proved the
power and grace of the Lord. "When I am
weak," he could say, "then I am strong"
(2 Cor. 12:10).

O, for this faith that accepts such afflictions
and persecutions as blessings in disguise – as
the means whereby the power and grace of
the Lord is experienced in mighty
deliverances.

Give me the faith to prove the truth of this verse, O Lord.
Amen.

Evening Reading: 2 Timothy 4

*"But the Lord stood with me and strengthened me . . .
[and] I was delivered." — 2 Timothy 4:17*

Here is a blessed verse for these days of real
trial. From verse 10, Paul enumerates some
very real trials that he was called to bear.
Yet in verse 17, he says, "But" or "in spite
of all," the Lord:

Stood with me. Not *by* me, but *with* me. There is
no trial or affliction in which He (Bless His
Name!) does not stand with *me*.

Strengthened me. "When I am weak, then I am
strong" (2 Cor. 12:10). His grace is sufficient
(see 2 Cor. 12:9). He not only stands with me,
but also strengthens my weakness.

Delivered me. He not only strengthens me, but
also saves me out of the mouth of the lion.

Praise His Holy Name!

"Rebuke them sharply." — Titus 1:13

Like the epistle to Timothy, this letter is an epistle to Titus giving teaching on the order, ordination, and organization in the church.

Titus was a young man. He was not as retiring and nervous as Timothy; in fact, he was of a more earnest, enthusiastic temperament. He was just the man for the Cretans and Corinthians to whom he was sent.

The Cretans, in particular, were "always liars, evil beasts, lazy gluttons" (v. 12). And it was among such people that Titus ministered for God. Paul, however, was confident in this young man of God and told him to go with all the authority of the Lord. No one was to despise his youth. He was to rebuke sharply if need be.

O Lord, let me be worthy of a similar power for You.
Amen.

"Exhort the young men to be sober-minded." — Titus 2:6

"Sober-minded" does not mean "long-faced" or "miserable." To be sober-minded means to be "temperate" or "level-headed."

If there is one danger in a young man's life, it is to be an extremist. This usually comes through lack of maturity and experience. And experience comes only through tribulation and patience. Thus, young men are exhorted to be sober-minded, capable of giving sound judgment and living temperately.

Notice it is "sober-minded." It is the mind or thoughts that eventually control one's life. If we are sober in thought, then we are sober in life.

Despite my youth, Lord, let me be Spirit-controlled and thus sober-minded.

"Reject a divisive man after the first and
second admonition." — Titus 3:10

One cannot drink poison, even if in small diluted doses, without being affected. This is true in the spiritual realm. A believer cannot read or talk about heresy without being in some measure affected. Thus, the apostle exhorts Titus (and Timothy as well; notice the first epistle) to shun foolish disputes, genealogies, strife, and fighting about the law because "they are unprofitable and useless" (v. 9).

The positive side is the better way, saturating oneself with pure truth.

He warns the young man Titus to avoid a divisive or heretical man after the first and second admonition. For such a man is perverted, sinful, and worst of all, self-condemned.

Help me, Lord, to recognize and avoid divisiveness
and heresy when confronted with it.

Evening Reading: Philemon 1

"Receive him as you would me." – Philemon 1:17

This letter presents a wonderful picture of Christ as the sinner's surety. For here, Paul pleads for Onesimus on the grounds of:

His Love. "I am sending him back. . . . My own heart" (v. 12). The heart was the seat of all affection in those days. And Paul implied in effect, "Receive him as you would receive my love."

His Person. "Receive him as you would me" (v. 17). The apostle here strips himself of all his righteousness as it were, and clothes the runaway slave with it by saying, "Receive him as you would me."

His Readiness to Repay for Anything Taken. "I will repay" (v. 19). Again, like my great surety, Paul promises to pay for the debt that was Onesimus' due.

How like Christ when He placed His mantle on us –
His love, His righteousness, His redemption!

"Upholding all things by the word of His power."
— Hebrews 1:3

It was through the Son that the creative Word was spoken: "'Let there be light'; and there was light" (Gen. 1:3). This verse teaches that it is similarly through the Son's Word of Power that all things are upheld or sustained.

God's principles that underlie the accomplishing of His purposes are ever the same. Thus, what was true of His creative work is true of His work of regeneration. The believing sinner is born again of the seed of the Word by the operation of the Holy Spirit. Similarly, he is sustained (upheld) by the same Word of His power.

The Word of God is the supreme means whereby the believer is sustained and empowered.

"Man shall not live by bread alone,
but by every word of God."
— Luke 4:4

"He is able to aid those who are tempted."
— Hebrews 2:18

The Darby translation renders this verse: "He is able to help those that are being tempted."[17]

He is able to help for "He Himself has suffered being tempted" (v. 18). He was, moreover, tempted in all points as we are, yet without sin.

Concerning temptation, James says, "Let no one say when he is tempted, 'I am tempted by God'; for God cannot be tempted by evil, nor does He Himself tempt anyone. But each one is tempted when he is drawn away by his own desires and enticed" (James 1:13-14).

"He is able to aid," for "no temptation has overtaken you except such as is common to man; but God is faithful, who will not allow you to be tempted beyond what you are able" (1 Cor. 10:13).

Thank You, Lord, for knowing temptation and guiding me through its snares.

"But exhort one another daily." — Hebrews 3:13

The proverbial saying is "Familiarity breeds contempt." But this is not true in the spiritual realm. At least, it is not true in the case of the spiritually-minded, because spiritual truths are inexhaustible, spiritual blessings unlimited, and the thoughts of God too vast to fully comprehend. So, there is a sense in which it is utterly impossible to become too familiar with spiritual things; there is always something new. This, however, is only true of the invisible and eternal.

On the other hand, to the carnal mind, spiritual things can become familiar. The obvious reason for this is that carnality in itself has brought the mind to a standstill, hence the stagnation.

Thus, the Word says that to avoid stagnation and to frustrate hardness of heart (through the deceitfulness of sin), "Exhort one another daily."

I pray, Lord, that I might encourage others,
just as You have sent others to exhort me.

"The word which they heard did not profit them,
not being mixed with faith in those who heard it."
— Hebrews 4:2

The Scriptures teach that "The just shall live
by faith" (Rom. 1:17, see also Hab. 2:4). In this
present age, the Christian life is a life of faith.
It was true as well of Old Testament saints
(Heb. 11). God honors faith. Faith touches the
invisible. Faith overlooks the concrete and
transient, and lays hold of God and His Word.
"Faith is the substance of things hoped for, the
evidence of things not seen" (Heb. 11:1).

Thus, the apostle points out the failure of the
children of Israel, who lost the blessing
because they did not accept God's Word with
positive faith. God honors faith like
Abraham's, for "He did not waver at the
promise of God" (Rom. 4:20).

"Lord, I believe; help my unbelief!"
— Mark 9:24

MORNING READING: HEBREWS 5

"Solid food belongs to those who are of full age, that is, those who by reason of use have their senses exercised to discern both good and evil." — Hebrews 5:14

The Word of God not only nourishes the soul, cleanses the life, and satisfies the mind, but it exercises the senses of the believer to discern good and evil.

Babes are partakers of milk and are inexperienced in the Word of Righteousness (or in right ways). Thus, spiritual babes are seen and found doing things that are contrary to the will of God, without any conscience of offense.

But for those who, by reason of this constant use of it, have become full grown men, there is the exercise of the senses. The implication here is that *sense*, under the control of the Holy Spirit, becomes a guide in the matters of good and evil, even when there is not definite teaching for or against any particular thing.

Blessed Lord, help me to "discern both good and evil."

"Do not become sluggish, but imitate those who through faith and patience inherit the promises."
— Hebrews 6:12

How comparatively easy it is to become a "sluggish" Christian! Sluggishness invites the believer to take the course of least resistance, to sit back and be an "armchair Christian," to just be content with the fact that the believer in Christ is secure and therefore there is no need for any exertion.

But Paul challenges such, and says, "Imitate those who through faith and patience inherit the promises." As to the promises, "Eye has not seen, nor ear heard, Nor have entered into the heart of man the things which God has prepared for those who love Him" (1 Cor. 2:9). These can all be inherited and experienced in faith, for "faith is the substance of things [patiently] hoped for" (Heb. 11:1).

Lord, may I demonstrate a faith that is both diligent and patient. Amen.

"There arises another priest who has come . . . according to the power of an endless life." — Hebrews 7:15-16

Those words in Revelation come home to me: "I am He who lives, and was dead, and behold, I am alive forevermore" (Rev. 1:18) – the Indissoluble Life.

He has conquered sin and death, and He lives evermore to reign. The grand thought here is this: Because He lives, I shall live. Because He possesses the indissoluble life, I too, possess it.

Notice the words: "the power of an endless life." He said of the resurrection, "All power is given unto me" (Matt. 28:18, KJV). It is the same power with which He indwells me. Thus the apostle says, "I live by faith in the Son of God, who loved me" (Gal. 2:20).

O Lord, deepen my experience of this life, for Your Name's sake. Amen.

"Make all things according to the pattern."
— Hebrews 8:5

These words were spoken to Moses. He had been alone in the mountain with God. He had seen the pattern of the tabernacle. He was now to reproduce it in the wilderness. Its reproduction in the wilderness became a means of infinite blessing to those Canaan-bound pilgrims.

The true tabernacle is Christ. Real visions of Him as such are only seen away in the Mount of Holy Communion with God. But when the great pattern is seen, the message comes to the believer, "Make all things [the light in the wilderness journey] according to the pattern."

O, that I might conform to the pattern of Christ!

"Without shedding of blood there is no remission."
— *Hebrews 9:22*

God is holy. He is of "purer eyes than to behold evil" (Hab. 1:13). If He is then to vindicate His holiness, He must punish sin, and punish it with death, "for the wages of sin is death" (Rom. 6:23) and "the soul who sins shall die" (Eze. 18:4).

God is also love. And while He hates sin, He loves the sinner. He made men for His pleasure, and His delights were always with the sons of men.

The question arises: How are these aspects of God's nature going to be reconciled? The answer that reverberates through the courts of heaven is that before the foundation of the world, God's well-beloved Son replied: "Here I am, send Me." And so He came, and bore in His own body our sin upon the tree. His shed blood satisfied God and provided remission for sins.

"Hallelujah! What a Savior!"[18]

"He who is coming will come and will not tarry."
— Hebrews 10:37

What a blessed hope! How it should purify
the heart even as He is pure.

"He who is coming will come and will not
tarry." The meaning here is undoubtedly the
same as that in the verse in Revelation: "Surely
I am coming quickly" (Rev. 22:20). It really
means, when He does come, He will come
quickly; there will be no tarrying. His coming
will be like lightning – suddenly, in a
moment, like a thief in the night. The hour
has merely to strike when He will suddenly
appear and events will follow with rapid
succession. He will not tarry. It will not be a
case of getting ready then.

O Lord, help me to live so as not to be ashamed!

Morning Reading: Hebrews 11

"Now faith is the substance of things hoped for,
the evidence of things not seen." – Hebrews 11:1

The truth of this verse is manifestly
demonstrated by the record of the men of
faith in this chapter of Hebrews.

"Faith is the substance of things hoped for." This is
best illustrated perhaps in the life of Abraham.
For "By faith Abraham obeyed when he was
called to go out to the place which he would
receive as an inheritance. And he went out,
not knowing where he was going" (v. 8). Here
was substance of things hoped. Elsewhere, it
is recorded of him that, "He did not waver at
the promise of God [an utter impossibility]
but was strengthened in faith" (Rom. 4:20). He
was rewarded.

"Faith is . . . the evidence of things not seen."
Here Moses perhaps best illustrates. "By faith
he forsook Egypt" (Heb. 11:27), with its
pleasures of sin, accounting the reproach of
Christ greater riches – assuring Him who is
invisible.

Lord, deepen my faith as You did for these men.

"Endure chastening." — Hebrews 12:7

O Lord, this is a message to my heart today, for I can say that my hands hang down and my knees are palsied. It seems to me that I am being chastened. For what, I do not really know. But Lord, I do know that it is for my good, and I would endure chastening until:

- I become a partaker of Your holiness.
- I yield peaceable fruit of righteousness.
- I am healed.

If this is the way to this threefold blessing, Lord, I will go all the way. So glorify Yourself in me for Your precious Name's sake.

Amen.

"The Lord is my helper; I will not fear." — Hebrews 13:6

What an encouraging verse this is! Solomon says, "The fear of man brings a snare" (Prov. 29:25). How true this is! Bondage to men because of fear is one of the greatest snares in a Christian's life. But this need not be if the heart is in the experience of this verse: "The Lord is my helper, I will not fear. What can man do to me?" (Heb. 13:6).

O, that I may enter into the practical experience of this verse; that I may be delivered from the fear of man. It would almost seem that Timothy suffered from the same things, for Paul writes to him, "Stir up the gift of God. . . . For God has not given us a spirit of fear, but of power and of love and of a sound mind. Therefore do not be ashamed of the testimony of our Lord" (2 Tim. 1:6-8).

The Lord is my Helper.

Evening Reading: James 1

*"Let every man be swift to hear, slow to speak,
slow to wrath." — James 1:19*

James' great theme is *Works*. He teaches that
faith without works is dead. He puts forward
the manward aspect of the Christian life,
emphasizing what the Lord said when He
gave utterance to these words, "By their fruits
you will know them" (Matt. 7:20). Thus, James'
epistle is one of practical religion.

Here are three practical truths:

Swift to Hear. Ready to hear. This is a thing
lacking in many lives: the readiness to hear.
How ready was the Lord Jesus!

Slow to Speak. This is, of course, in proportion
to hearing. One should always be more ready
to hear than to speak.

Slow to Wrath. Hastiness! But James says,
"The wrath of man does not produce the
righteousness of God" (James 1:20).

*O, that my life and testimony
would be known by these truths. Amen.*

MORNING READING: JAMES 2

"Fulfill the royal law." — James 2:8

The royal law is defined thus: "You shall love
your neighbor as yourself" (v. 8). And it is the
command that the Lord Jesus pointed out as
including all other commandments. Of
course, this command implies love to God
first, and then love to man. James points out
that the fulfilling of it is the hallmark of
kingship or royalty. So that if I am a genuine
king and priest to God, I am one who fulfills
this command.

He goes further to explain that he who shows
partiality and who breaks this royal law
commits sin. "God shows no partiality" (Acts
10:34); so why should we? Whether poor or
rich, they should be loved, honored, and
recognized without partiality.

No wonder the Lord Jesus was the Friend of
Sinners!

Teach me to love others as You love me, Lord.

"If anyone does not stumble in word, he is a perfect man."
— James 3:2

The verses that follow describe with great eloquence something of the power and affect of an uncontrolled tongue. James goes on to say that while animals, birds, creeping things, and things in the sea can be tamed, "no man can tame the tongue" (vv. 7-8).

Praise God, Christ can tame the tongue! Moreover, He can control it after it is tamed.

The Lord spoke as no man had spoken. Wonderful words proceeded out of His mouth. People wondered at His gracious words. He is just the same today, and He indwells me! O, to be controlled by Him.

Lord, I submit my tongue to be tamed
and controlled by You. Amen.

MORNING READING: JAMES 4

MORNING READING: JAMES 4

*"Humble yourselves in the sight of the Lord,
and He will lift you up."* — James 4:10

Promotion comes by way of deepest
humiliation. This was true of the Lord Jesus,
and it is true of all who have been exalted by
God.

Philippians 2:8-11: "He humbled Himself and
became obedient to the point of death, even
the death of the cross. Therefore God also has
highly exalted Him and given Him the name
which is above every name, that at the name
of Jesus every knee should bow . . . and that
every tongue should confess that Jesus Christ
is Lord, to the glory of God the Father."

If ever Christ is going to be exalted in my life,
it is when I humble myself "to the point of
death, even the death of the cross." When the
cross and its shame and suffering come deeply
into my life, and the flesh in me is crucified,
then Christ will live.

Humble me then, O Lord. Bend me!

*"My brethren, take the prophets, who spoke in the name
of the Lord, as an example of suffering and patience."*
— James 5:10

Was it not Hudson Taylor who told a young
candidate for the mission field that there were
three very important lessons to learn in God's
work? The first was patience; the second was
patience; and the third was patience.

Paul says that tribulation works patience.
This was undoubtedly true in Job's case. He
certainly suffered affliction! And so did many
prophets who spoke in the name of the Lord.

*Lord, if I should have to pass by way of tribulation,
I do pray that I may learn the lesson of patience.*

Morning Reading: 1 Peter 1

"Since you have purified your souls in obeying the truth through the Spirit in sincere love." — 1 Peter 1:22

The two greatest things which should characterize Christians are purified souls and unfeigned love. The secret of both of these is in the obeying of the truth through the Spirit.

I take this as a work which the Holy Spirit affects in the heart of the believer when there is true obedience to the truth revealed. First, I see a truth; next, I obey it in the power of the Spirit; finally, it is made real and living to me by the Spirit. All this results in purifying my life and thus begetting an unfeigned love.

Without holiness, no man shall see God. He says, "Be holy, for I am holy" (Lev. 11:45). Then, "Whoever does not practice righteousness is not of God, nor is he who does not love his brother. . . . Love one another" (1 John 3:10-11).

Lord, help me to remember that it is not true because it is real to me, but rather it is real because it is True!

Evening Reading: 1 Peter 2

"As free, yet not using liberty as a cloak for vice, but as bondservants of God. Honor all people. Love the brotherhood. Fear God. Honor the king." — 1 Peter 2:16-17

Note the order in verse 17: first, honor all men; second, love the brotherhood; third, fear God; and fourth, honor the king.

And while subjecting myself to "every ordinance of man for the Lord's sake" (v. 13), living as free, yet not having the freedom for a cloak of wickedness, but as bondservants of God (see v. 16).

This is why Paul, though he was a man who recognized and acknowledged the ordinances of men, could boldly say, "We ought to obey God rather than men" (Acts 5:29). He was ready to obey insofar as their commands were not contrary to the dictates of God.

O Lord, enable me to use my freedom rightly.

"Be ready to give a defense to everyone who asks you a reason for the hope that is in you." — 1 Peter 3:15

The "blessed man" of Psalm 1 is said to be "like a tree planted by the rivers of water, that brings forth its fruit in its season" (Ps. 1:3) – always ready to give an answer concerning the hope that is in him, "Christ in you, the hope of glory" (Col. 1:27). Readiness to witness of the indwelling Christ will be seen in:

A *zeal for that which is good.* It could be said of the Lord Jesus: "Zeal for Your house has eaten me up" (Ps. 69:9).

A *willingness to suffer for righteousness' sake.* Walking "in the paths of righteousness for His name's sake" (Ps. 23:3).

Sanctifying the Lord as Christ in the heart. Making Christ supreme in life. Owning Him as Lord. Sanctifying or setting Him aside as the only One worthy to reign supreme in the heart. Undivided allegiance.

Lord, help me to be ever prepared.
The next person I meet may need You!

"That in all things God may be glorified
through Jesus Christ." — 1 Peter 4:11

This paragraph is most instructive. It gives in
a concise form just what the duty of the
believer is and with what objective all should
be done. After exhorting to soberness, love,
soundness of mind, and prayerfulness, Peter
goes on to enumerate the following
responsibilities:

1. Using hospitality.
2. Ministering gifts.
3. Speaking the oracles of God.
4. Ministering as the strength is supplied.

And all this for the glory of God through
Jesus Christ!

So, Lord, make these four necessary things living in my
experience that I may glorify You. Amen.

*"The devil walks about like a roaring lion, seeking whom
he may devour. Resist him, steadfast in the faith."*
— 1 Peter 5:8-9

The apostle John writes, "This is the victory
that has overcome the world – our faith"
(1 John 5:4). A little before this, he explains
the *world* is: "the lust of the flesh, the lust of
the eyes, and the pride of life" (1 John 2:16). In
other words, it is the internal foe, the external
foe, and the infernal foe. And the victory
which overcomes this trinity of evil is
"The Faith."

Faith touches the invisible; calls those things
which are not as though they are; laughs at
impossibilities and cries, "It shall be done."
Faith *claims* (all the power of a risen Christ);
commands (the mountains of spiritual barriers
to be removed and they are removed); and
conquers (Heb. 11 – this is the victory, even
your faith).

*Lord, teach me to rely on the power of faith
for victory against evil.*

"Exceedingly great and precious promises." — 2 Peter 1:4

"For whatever things were written before were written for our learning, that we through the patience and comfort of the Scriptures might have hope" (Rom. 15:4). "For all the promises of God in Him are Yes, and in Him Amen, to the glory of God through us" (2 Cor. 1:20).

How grand it is to be able to claim such promises as are revealed in this grand Book. And to claim them in positive faith too – even as did Abraham, for he staggered not at the promises of God through unbelief, but was strong in faith, "being fully convinced that what [God] had promised He was able also to perform" (Rom. 4:21).

Faith makes the promises realities.

O, to enter into the blessings of God's promises now, Lord.

Morning Reading: 2 Peter 2

"For if, after they have escaped the pollutions of the world through the knowledge of the Lord and Savior Jesus Christ, they are again entangled in them and overcome, the latter end is worse for them than the beginning."
— 2 Peter 2:20

The whole of this chapter is very much like many of the parentheses of Hebrews. Here, Peter describes the character and practices of a false prophet. But the most striking verse is the one quoted above. Though obviously not born-again, it is possible for such a man to escape the pollutions of the world – through the knowledge (intellectual knowledge, not experiential knowledge) of the Lord and Savior Jesus Christ. Just as salt preserves in the midst of corruption, so the knowledge of Christ preserves a man from the pollution of the world. But if not born-again, the end of such a person is worse than for the ignorant sinner.

Lord, help me bring those with intellectual knowledge into relational experience.

"The Lord is not slack concerning His promise."
— 2 Peter 3:9

Jesus is coming, is coming again!
Jesus is coming again!
Shout the glad tidings
O'er mountain and plain!
Jesus is coming again![19]

Here is a very stirring message. Peter had to stir his readers up in remembrance of the great fact that Jesus was coming again. With the elapse of time, many were getting weary and asking such questions as "Where is the promise of His coming?" Thus, the apostle answers with these words: "The Lord is not slack concerning His promise."

Lord, keep me ever watching for Your return,
for Your Name's sake.

"That which was from the beginning, which we have heard, which we have seen with our eyes, which we have looked upon, and our hands have handled, concerning the Word of life." — 1 John 1:1

The human being possesses five senses: sight, smell, feel, taste, and hearing. Of these five, three are particularly useful for making contact with a person. One would hardly smell or taste a person, but one would certainly hear, see, and handle a person.

Thus, John uses these three in particular to illustrate the intimacy of this relationship with the Lord Jesus, proving, of course, the fact that Christ was Jesus (human) and One with whom real spiritual and human fellowship was enjoyed.

Through these same three, but now spiritual senses, Christ may still be made real to me through spiritual vision (sight) and faith (hands and hearing).

Heighten my spiritual senses, Lord,
that I might have true intimacy with You.

"Whoever keeps His word, truly the love of God is perfected in him." — 1 John 2:5

"Perfect love casts out fear" (1 John 4:18). Love as I have seen in past quiet times is the "more excellent way" (1 Cor. 12:31). It is the sum and total of all that is spiritual, "for God is love" (1 John 4:8).

In this verse, John says, "Whoever keeps His word, truly the love of God is perfected in him." Thus, the secret of perfect love in the experience of the Christian is the keeping of God's Word. The Lord Jesus said, "If you love Me, keep My commandments" (John 14:15).

O Lord, give me the needed grace to keep Your Word and obey Your commands, that Your love may be perfected in me.

*"Whatever we ask we receive from Him, because
we keep His commandments and do those things that
are pleasing in His sight." — 1 John 3:22*

Previously, I learned that the condition for
perfected love in me was keeping God's Word.
Here, the condition for answered prayers is
keeping His commandments. John is no
doubt quoting from the words to which the
Lord Jesus gave utterance in those last
discourses before He left for the cross and
then the glory: "If you abide in Me, and My
words abide in you, you will ask what you
desire, and it shall be done for you" (John
15:7); "And whatever you ask in My name, that
I will do, that the Father may be glorified in
the Son" (John 14:13).

The four conditions for answered prayer are:
- Keeping God's Word
- Seeking God's Will
- Seeking God's Glory
- Pleading Christ's Name.

*May I always consider my fulfillment of these conditions,
Lord, before coming to Your throne.*

"He who is in you is greater than he who is in the world."
— 1 John 4:4

Here is a marvelous thing – that in *me* is a power vested in a person that is greater than he (the Devil and all his powers) that is in the world!

The chapter goes on to reveal that I am indwelt by the Godhead (Christ and the Holy Spirit): "By this we know that we abide in Him, and He in us, because He has given us of His Spirit" (v. 13). Notice also v. 16: "He who abides in love abides in God, and God in him." Here is a verse that shows that God indwells me. Actually, the fact that I am indwelt by the Trinity is a truth that the Lord Jesus taught (see John 14). That is to say, that potentially I am indwelt by the eternal power and Godhead.

Who is he that can stand against me?

Thank You, Lord, that I am never alone, especially when I face the enemy who hates me because You indwell me!

Morning Reading: 1 John 5

"If we ask anything according to His will, He hears us."
— 1 John 5:14

I had a quiet time on a similar verse only the other day; but the message of *Power in Prayer* has gripped me once again.

Notice the verse that follows the one quoted above: "Whatever we ask, we know that we have the petitions that we have asked of Him" (v. 16).

To know that the "whatever" is the will of God is to know that I have the petitions that I desired of Him. It only requires the taking of positive faith.

I have seen already that the great divine principle in creation, in redemption, in the believer, etc. is that God thinks (His will), the Son speaks, and the Spirit produces. If I know His will, the rest of that principle is worked out in my life. Blessed fact!

Thy will be done, Lord. Amen.

Evening Reading: 2 John 1

"If anyone comes to you and does not bring this doctrine,
do not receive him into your house nor greet him; for he
who greets him shares in his evil deeds."
— 2 John 1:10-11

The heretics that John writes about in these
verses were those who deliberately went
about teaching "Antichrist" doctrines. The
greeting was not the formal greeting of today,
but one of identification and brotherhood.
And the apostle warns the elect lady, who was
probably the owner of a rest house, not to
identify herself with heresy by seeking God's
blessing upon the heretics.

This, however, in no way cuts across the
believer's privilege to make known the truth
wherever there is the opportunity. The Lord
says, "If anyone [or church] . . . opens the door,
I will come in" (Rev. 3:20).

Protect Your truth in my heart, Lord,
that it might never mingle with the enemy's lies.

"Imitate . . . what is good." — 3 John 1:11

The apostle John was writing to Gaius, an upright, spiritual, and loving man. He first rejoices in the character and conduct of Gaius, and then writes rebukingly of Diotrephes, "who loves to have the preeminence" among men (v. 9). Of this man, the apostle says some very scathing things.

John knew very well that in all things there was only One who was entitled to preeminence, and that was the Lord Jesus. Thus, contrasting Diotrephes with the Lord, he calls one evil and the other good. There is one that is good, and that is God. He therefore sums up his letter by exhorting Gaius to "imitate . . . what is good."

O Lord, help me to ever follow and imitate You
in definite preference to a Diotrephes.

"Praying in the Holy Spirit." — Jude 1:20

Herein lies the secret of effectual prayer. "Likewise the Spirit also helps in our weaknesses. For we do not know what we should pray for as we ought, but the Spirit Himself makes intercession for us with groanings which cannot be uttered. . . . He makes intercession for the saints according to the will of God" (Rom. 8:26-27).

So praying in the Holy Spirit really means:
- Guided Prayer (Rom. 8:27)
- God's Will in Prayer (Rom. 8:27)
- Effectual Fervent Prayer (Rom. 8:26)

How necessary then to pray in the Holy Spirit!

Teach me more, O Lord, of this kind of prayer. Amen.

"I am He who lives, and was dead, and behold, I am alive forevermore. Amen. And I have the keys of Hades and of Death." – Revelation 1:18

"I *am He who lives*." "In Him was life, and the life was the light of men" (John 1:4). This speaks of His eternity. He is from "everlasting to everlasting" (Ps. 90:2).

"I . . . *was dead*." "Christ died for our sins according to the Scriptures" (1 Cor. 15:3). This speaks of His atoning work.

"I *am alive forevermore*." He now lives in "the power of an endless life" (Heb. 7:16). "Knowing that Christ, having been raised from the dead, dies no more. Death no longer has dominion over Him" (Rom. 6:9).

"I *have the keys*" – of Heaven and of Hell (only He could unlock the gate of heaven and let us in). He holds the issues of men's lives in His hand. For the Father has handed all judgment over to the Son. He holds the keys – the symbol of power and sovereignty. He holds the keys of every kingdom, problem, and situation.

Thank God, He lives in me.

"You have left your first love." – *Revelation* 2:4

The church in Ephesus failed in all when she failed in love. For *love* is the all-inclusive word which embraces all other fruits of the Spirit.

The Lord had to say to this church:

"I *know your works*" (v. 2). Here was the work of faith. In faith, this church was strong. Then again:

"I *know your patience*" (v. 2). Here was the patience of hope. In hope, this church was strong.

But the Lord goes on to say, "I have this against you, that you have left your first love" (v. 4). Here the church had failed, and therefore failed in all. For while these three remain – faith, hope, and love – "the greatest of these is love" (1 Cor. 13:13). The other two are comprehended in love, and Ephesus had failed here.

O Lord, help me not to fail in love.

"See, I have set before you an open door,
and no one can shut it." — Revelation 3:8

These words were written to the church in
Philadelphia. But they are words that can be
appropriated today without doing injustice to
the context. When the Lord opens a door – no
one can shut it! What a grand thought! There
are three reasons given which form the basis
of an open door:

"You have a little strength" (v. 8). All power
belongs to Christ. He said this on that great
Ascension Day. When He gives the power, He
opens the door for the use of it.

"You . . . have kept My word" (v. 8). Here is
another condition for an open door – the
keeping of God's Word. God always honors
the servant who is faithful to the Word, with
an open door.

"You . . . have not denied My name" (v. 8). If we
deny Him, He will deny us. If we suffer, we
shall reign.

O, to have the eye to see the doors
of opportunity which the Lord opens.

"You are worthy, O Lord, to receive glory and honor and power; for You created all things, and by Your will they exist and were created." — Revelation 4:11

I have been created, and am now living, for the pleasure (and by the will) of God if these three characteristics are true of me:

He is worthy to receive glory. My life should have as its first characteristic the glorifying of God. The Lord says in John 15:8, "By this My Father is glorified, that you bear much fruit," the fruit of character.

He is worthy to receive honor. Here is the second characteristic: to give God honor is to give Him His due. He is worthy of all.

He is worthy to receive power. Thirdly, power. Not only what He does in me and what I am, but also He is worthy to receive what I can do!

May all that I am and all that I do bring You glory and honor and power. Amen.

"The Lion . . . has prevailed." – Revelation 5:5

John says, "I wept much, because no one was found worthy to open and read the scroll, or to look at it" (v. 4). And well might he weep, for the solution to the universal problem lay in the unsealing of this book.

But John records, "the Lion of the tribe of Judah . . . has prevailed." He prevailed when He fought and won that greatest of all battles at the Cross of Calvary.

On the basis of that same victory, all books, all seals can now be opened. Books and seals of problems in my life present no problem now to Him, for He has prevailed.

O Lord, teach me how to appropriate the fruits of Your death in everyday life. Amen.

EVENING READING: REVELATION 6

"Those who had been slain for the word of God and for the testimony which they held." – Revelation 6:9

How true this has been right down through the ages, and it is yet to be repeated! Men and women of God, who have turned the world right side up, have suffered at the hands of their persecutors to the point of death. Notice, they were:

Slain for the Word of God. "Heaven and earth will pass away, but My words will by no means pass away," said the Lord Jesus (Matt. 24:35). The Word of God – nothing but that! O, to be a defender of this precious Word.

Slain also for their testimony. What testimonies they will have. Nothing superficial. Testimonies born of a real experience of God!

Lord, grant me grace and strength should this ever be my calling. Meanwhile, may my testimony be of a real experience of God!

Morning Reading: Revelation 7

*"They shall neither hunger anymore nor thirst anymore;
the sun shall not strike them, nor any heat."*
— Revelation 7:16

This is going to be the enjoyed portion of all
the God-fearing people who shall come out of
the great tribulation (v. 14).

Actually, this will be the experience of all who
dwell in the presence of Christ, for there is no
such thing as hunger, thirst, or weariness in
His presence. When here on earth Jesus said,
"He who comes to Me shall never hunger, and
he who believes in Me shall never thirst"
(John 6:35). He also said, "Come to Me, all you
who labor and are heavy laden" (Matt. 11:28)
– those laboring under the scorching heat of
the sun and sin. And in a measure, all true
believers experience the truth of the above
verse even now.

*O Lord, how much more so will we experience these
truths when we are in those bright realms of bliss!*

"When He opened the seventh seal . . ." — Revelation 8:1

This chapter, like the many to come, reveals a portion of what is actually going to take place on earth when God judges the rebellious people.

The writer to the Hebrews tells his readers two things in particular about God in one of the chapters. First, that "God is a consuming fire" (Heb. 12:29). His holiness and righteous judgment on all sin demands this aspect of His nature. And thus, it is not remarkable that such a chapter as this is written to illustrate, or better demonstrate, what God is going to do with and among those who deliberately leave Him out of their lives now. Secondly, that "it is a fearful thing to fall into the hands of the living God" (Heb. 10:31). This, of course, is His judicial hand.

I do praise You, Father,
that I will never have to be judged for sin!

"To them was given power." — Revelation 9:3

In the light of this chapter and particularly this verse, it is wonderful to see how God in His matchless omnipotence uses whomsoever and whatsoever He pleases to execute His purposes.

If He can use a scorpion, why not me? Here He uses the scorpions of the earth. Power is given them to *harm* but not to *kill*. They are not to touch or hurt anything or anyone except those who do not carry the seal of God on their foreheads. They are to torment for five months and then to cease tormenting. The torment is "like the torment of a scorpion when it strikes a man" (v. 5). I, myself, have undergone the torture of being struck by a scorpion. For twenty-four hours, I experienced "hell." Finally, through sheer exhaustion I became unconscious until the worst pain was over. It is no wonder that the tormented in that day will "seek death and . . . will desire to die," but "death will flee from them" (v. 6).

O Lord, help me to convey the coming torment
so that others may avoid it.

*"Take and eat it [the little book]; and it will make
your stomach bitter, but it will be as sweet as honey
in your mouth." — Revelation 10:9*

The Word of God is very often sweet to the
spiritual taste, but very bitter to the flesh.
How often one speaks of a promise being
sweet, but how different it is to enter into the
experiential knowledge of it! For very often,
to experience such a promise, the flesh has to
be drastically dealt with.

Faith is the soul's taste, while the belly speaks
of that which is carnal and very often
intemperate. It was said of some that their
"god is their belly" (Phil. 3:19).

But bitter or not, the command to John and to
me is "Take it up and eat it."

*O, that I may withstand the bitter in order to fully
appreciate the sweetness of Your promises.*

"These are the two olive trees, and the two lampstands standing before the God of the earth." – Revelation 11:4

This verse describes the two witnesses of verse three. Their names are not disclosed, but many think that one of them will be Elijah.

It is interesting to study the significance of the two things in particular that are given to describe them:

Two lampstands. Like John the Baptist, and believers today, they will be the "lamps" of the world, shining for God upon earth. What a wonderful ministry to fulfill!

Two olive trees. This is a picture of the Holy Spirit who will indwell them to fill their lamps with oil. The power to shine, to shut heaven, and to smite the earth will be given to them by the Holy Spirit.

"You are the light of the world. . . . Let your light so shine before men, that they may see your good works and glorify your Father in heaven."
– Matthew 5:14, 16

"Her Child was caught up to God." — Revelation 12:6

I see here the triumph of Christ over sin, Satan, and death. Surely, the picture here is that of the Lord Jesus in His birth, life, death, and resurrection. Though the dragon was there to swallow Him up, yet He became victorious over death.

"Up from the grave He arose
With a mighty triumph o'er His foes."[20]

Through this victory, the angels and Michael were able to overcome the Devil. "They overcame [the Devil] by the blood of the Lamb and by the word of their testimony" (v. 11).

*Lord, make real to me more of the victory of
Your death and risen life. Amen.*

"I saw a beast." – Revelation 13:1

It is interesting to notice the trinity of evil as it is revealed in this chapter.

The beast of verse one, it seems, is the Antichrist. Notice, in verse three, he will appear as one who was slain but now risen. What a counterfeit!

In verse two, it appears the dragon here is the Anti-God. He will be vested with the power and authority of government – the power, moreover, to impart power. A counterfeit of God.

In verse 11, this beast (the False Prophet) will falsely represent the Holy Spirit.

Thus, the Devil will see to it in that day that his infernal trinity will unite together to resist the power, truth, and life of God, the Son, and the Holy Spirit. What a grand day when He that will come shall come to destroy His foes!

*O, for the day when I will witness
the victory of the true Trinity!*

EVENING READING: REVELATION 14

*"These are the ones who follow the Lamb
wherever He goes."* — Revelation 14:4

Such is John's description of the 144,000 true
believers in the coming day of tribulation.
Actually, they are the spiritual remnant from
among the Jews. There are three things in
particular said of these godly people:

They Were Purchased. "These were redeemed
from among men, being firstfruits to God and
to the Lamb" (v. 4), bought by the precious
blood of Christ.

They Were Pure. In character, they were pure:
"In their mouth was found no deceit" (v. 5),
"they are virgins" (v. 4). In conduct, they were
pure: "They are without fault" (v. 5), "these are
the ones who were not defiled with women"
(v. 4).

They Were Partisans. "These are the ones who
follow the Lamb wherever He goes" (v. 4).

Lord, make this threefold testimony true of me. Amen.

*"They sing the song of Moses, the servant of God,
and the song of the Lamb" — Revelation 15:3*

It is beautiful to see that the song of these
redeemed and sheltered Hebrews concerns
none other than the Lamb. They sing not of
their own courage, fidelity, and endurance in
suffering and death (though they shall suffer
as no one humanly speaking has ever
suffered), but they sing of the power and
glory of the Lamb.

What height of spirituality is this! How
pleasing to God! For then no suffering, no
trial would ever dim the joy that is set before
the truly spiritual Christian who has his
vision filled with the glory of the Lamb.
Christ Himself endured the cross despising
the shame because of the joy that was set
before Him. Paul says that he reckons "that
the sufferings of this present time are not
worthy to be compared with the glory which
shall be revealed in us" (Rom. 8:18).

*O, that this principle would be true
in my experience, Lord.*

"Men blasphemed God because of the plague of the hail."
— *Revelation 16:21*

One of the most amazing things about the judgments that are foretold in this Book is that they enrage those upon whom they fall to an even greater degree. Notice especially the seventeenth chapter.

Of course, the people upon whom these judgments will come will be "vessels of wrath prepared for destruction" (Rom. 9:22), those who have deliberately chosen to rebel against God. Thus, like Esau, though they should seek repentance with tears, they would not repent.

But in spite of this, it is very important to note that the negative side of the revelation of God very rarely turns man to repentance. On the other hand, "the goodness of God leads [men] to repentance" (Rom. 2:4).

O, that I might reach men with the goodness of God
before they become the focus of the judgment of God.

"Those who are with Him are called, chosen, and faithful." – Revelation 17:14

The victory of the Lamb over the "the great whore" (v. 1) is going to be won with the cooperation of godly Jews whom He is going to call, choose, and depend upon. The great whore is the final development of corrupt and Christ-less religion.

Surely, a lesson can be learned from this future victory. For this is a victory to be won now; and that in the same sphere – the sphere of so-called Christendom. The qualifications necessary for the fighting line are:

The Assurance of Having Been Called. This is an inward work of the Holy Spirit. O, to make sure of this calling and election!

The Assurance of Having Been Chosen. One can be called and yet not be chosen. Christ chose His own because they answered the call.

Faithfulness – The all-inclusive requirement.

It is Your calling, Your choice, and Your faithfulness that works in me to bring You glory. Glorify Thyself, Lord!

"Babylon the great is fallen." — Revelation 18:2

This chapter is taken up with the fall of the "Great Babylon." The picture portrayed is vivid.

The great city decked like a queen with rich apparel; a monument of earthly achievement; and yet a cesspool of sinful corruption. This city, many years in building and development, is pictured here in destruction. Indeed, total destruction – the judgment of one single day.

How like the house that was built upon the sinking sands of time! How futile to build for time! It is only the enjoyment of a mere season. How the merchants and lovers of this city weep, cry, and mourn the fate of their much-loved city!

Thank You, Lord, for that city not made with hands,
eternal in the heavens, and reserved for me.

"I heard a loud voice of a great multitude in heaven,
saying, 'Alleluia!'" — Revelation 19:1

The word "Alleluia" occurs both in the Old Testament and in the New Testament. The four times the word is used in the New Testament are all in this passage.

Alleluia means, "Praise ye Jehovah." And it is a very apt note of praise in the light of this passage. The harlot will have been defeated and destroyed, the Marriage Supper of the Lamb spread, and the partakers thereof, full of the joy of God's Salvation, will proclaim, "Alleluia!"

This is a word which should give expression to the experience that follows every defeat of the Devil in the believer's life. In trial or in pain; in joy or in triumph, the true believer ought to say, "Alleluia!"

O, to know more of the Alleluia Life!

EVENING READING: REVELATION 20

"I saw a great white throne." – Revelation 20:11

What a vision for the Apostle John to see!
What a vision it will be when both small and
great will one day have to stand before this
"Great White Throne" to be judged according
to their works! It will be such an awe-
inspiring sight that earth and heaven will flee
away from the face of the One who shall sit
upon the throne.

Great – because of the Person who will be
enthroned upon this throne – He whom God
has ordained to judge the world.

White – because of the purity of the One who
shall sit upon the throne. He is the Holy One.

Throne – because of the power of the One who
shall occupy the throne.

"When the Son of Man comes in His glory,
and all the holy angels with Him, then He will
sit on the throne of His glory."
– Matthew 25:31

Morning Reading: Revelation 21

*"The holy Jerusalem, descending out of heaven
from God." — Revelation 21:10*

What a beautiful picture is presented here of
the heavenly Jerusalem! O, the glory, majesty,
and mystery of it!

As to size, the height, breadth, and width alike
will be 1,400 miles! It will be made of pure
gold. The foundations will be made of the
most precious stones. The gates will be
perpetually open, for there will be no night in
which to close them. The glory of God will
lighten it, and the Lamb the Light thereof.
There will be no temple in it because the
Almighty and the Lamb are the temple of it.

Its subjects will only be those whose names
will be found written in the Lamb's Book of
Life. Nothing that defiles will ever enter
there.

*O worship, my soul, that I have been made
an inheritor of such mysteries!*

"Behold, I am coming quickly." —*Revelation 22:7*

This beautiful expression lays emphasis on three great things that are the believer's portion when Christ comes quickly. The word "behold" calls attention to these.

"Behold, I am coming quickly! Blessed is he who keeps the words of the prophecy" (v. 7). Christ's coming is going to be a time of rejoicing. It will be blessed for those who keep the sayings of God.

"Behold, I am coming quickly, and My reward is with Me" (v. 12). Christ's coming is going to be a time of rewarding. This also calls the believers' attention!

"'Surely I am coming quickly.' Amen. Even so, come, Lord Jesus!" (v. 20). The word "surely" is a much stronger word. Of all facts, this is the greatest. *"This same Jesus, who was taken up from you into heaven, will so come in like manner as you saw Him go into heaven"* (Acts 1:11). What a blessed certainty!

Help me to always be ready, watchful, and busy about my Father's business, for in the twinkling of an eye . . .

ENDNOTES

1 "O For a Closer Walk with God." Hymn. Words by William Cowper, 1731-1800.

2 *The Holy Bible: New Translation*. (London: G. Morrish, 1920), Matthew 26:49.

3 "When I Survey the Wondrous Cross." Hymn. Words by Isaac Watts, 1674-1748.

4 "Jesus Is All the World to Me." Hymn. Words and music by Will L. Thompson, 1847-1909.

5 "'Man of Sorrows,' What a Name." Hymn. Words and music by Phillip P. Bliss, 1838-1876.

6 T. L. Hargrave.

7 "Turn Your Eyes upon Jesus." Hymn. Words and music by Helen H. Lemmel, 1864-1961.

8 "A Charge to Keep I Have." Hymn. Words by Charles Wesley, 1707-1788.

9 *The Holy Bible: New Translation*. (London: G. Morrish, 1920), John 2:17.

10 "Amazing Grace! How Sweet the Sound." Hymn. Words by John Newton, 1725-1807.

11 "God Moves in a Mysterious Way." Hymn. Words by William Cowper, 1731-1800.

12 "When I Survey the Wondrous Cross." Hymn. Words by Isaac Watts, 1674-1748.

13 "Take My Life and Let it Be." Hymn. Words by Frances R. Havergal, 1836-1879.

14 "On His Blindness." Sonnet by John Milton, 1608-1674, line 14.

15 "Grace Greater than Our Sin." Hymn. Words by Julia H. Johnston, 1849-1919.

16 "I Worship Thee, Sweet Will of God." Hymn. Words by Frederick W. Faber, 1814-1863.

17 *The Holy Bible: New Translation.* (London: G. Morrish, 1920), Hebrews 2:18.

18 "'Man of Sorrows,' What a Name." Hymn. Words and music by Phillip P. Bliss, 1838-1876.

19 "Jesus is Coming." Hymn. Words by Daniel W. Whittle, 1840-1901.

20 "Low in the Grave He Lay." Hymn. Words and music by Robert Lowry, 1826-1899.